LET THEM

Eat

Cake

and other Low-Fat and Low-Cholesterol Desserts

VIRGINIA N. WHITE

with Rosa A. Mo, R.D.

Let Them Eat Cake
®1992
by Virginia N. White

Library of Congress Cataloging-in-Publication Data

White, Virginia N.
      Let them eat cake: and other low-fat and low-cholesterol
            desserts / Virginia N. White with Rosa A. Mo.
                p.   cm.
      Includes index.
      ISBN 1-56561-001-3 : $12.95
      1. Low-fat diet--Recipes. 2. Low-cholesterol diet--Recipes.
      3. Desserts.
 I. Mo, Rosa A.   II. Title
RM237.7.W48   1992
641.8'6--dc20   92-26428
                                     CIP

Edited by Donna Hoel
Cover Design by Terry Dugan
Production Coordinator by Claire Lewis
Printed in the United States of America

10 9 8 7 6 5 4 3 2 1

Published by: CHRONIMED Publishing
P.O. Box 47945
Minneapolis, MN 55447-9727

Let Them Eat Cake
•••••••••••••••

DEDICATION

*This book is dedicated
to my three favorite taste testers:
Rick, Christy, and Julie.*

Let Them Eat Cake
● ● ● ● ● ● ● ● ● ● ● ● ● ● ● ● ●

ACKNOWLEDGMENTS

In 1985 I began inventing recipes to help my husband with his cholesterol problem. He was so pleased with the results that he urged me to collect the recipes and write a cookbook. I am ever grateful to him for that suggestion, but most of all for believing I could do it. All my thanks go to him for his constant support, good humor (especially when the computer was not working), enthusiastic help, and eager appetite.

My daughters, Christy and Julie, also deserve a lot of credit for their willingness to try out everything I served them. Not every experiment was a success, and they were the ones that had to find that out.

A heartfelt thanks goes to my friends and family for their ideas, suggestions, adaptable recipes, and eagerness to test my experiments.

Thank you to everyone at CHRONIMED Publishing, especially David Wexler for his support and enthusiasm.

Special thanks to Rosa Mo for all her excellent advice. It was a pleasure working with Rosa and everyone else who contributed to this book.

NUTRITIONAL ANALYSIS

The analytic software used for the nutritional breakdown of these recipes is Auto-Nutritionist III, Version 7.0.

In many of the recipes you can choose which ingredients to use to fit your needs, how much of the ingredient to use to suit your palate, how big or small the serving size to satisfy your appetite, or whether to use an ingredient at all.

The following guidelines are used in the analysis:

Where there is a choice of ingredients in the recipe, the item chosen for the nutritional analysis is the one with the most calories. For example, if a recipe calls for apple juice or orange juice or water, the item analyzed is apple juice, which has the most calories.

If the choice of ingredients does not differ calorically, the item chosen for the nutritional analysis is the one mentioned in the recipe instructions or the one with the highest saturated fat content. For example, if a recipe gives you a choice of canola oil, light-tasting peanut oil, or a vegetable oil low in saturated fat such as corn oil, the item analyzed is peanut oil, which has 18% saturated fat. Canola oil has only 6% saturated fat, while corn oil has 13%.

If the choice is in the amount of the individual ingredient, the greater amount is used to analyze the recipe's nutritional value. For example, you can choose from a minimum of 1/3 cup to a maximum of 1/2 cup of brown sugar depending on your taste. The maximum amount is used for the nutritional analysis.

You can choose to get 6 to 8 servings from a recipe. The smaller yield is used so the larger serving size is analyzed.

All optional ingredients are included in the recipe analysis.

The nutritional values, therefore, are the maximum you will consume. If you decide to choose a low-calorie alternative, an oil with less saturated fat, a smaller amount, or not use an ingredient at all, you will be eating less than the amounts given in the nutritional breakdown.

ENJOY!

Let Them Eat Cake
• • • • • • • • • • • • • • • •

TABLE OF CONTENTS

Let Them Eat Cake
•••••••••••••••

Let Them Eat Cake
• • • • • • • • • • • • • •

Let Them Eat Cake
• • • • • • • • • • • • • • • •

Let Them Eat Cake
● ● ● ● ● ● ● ● ● ● ● ● ● ● ● ●

Let Them Eat Cake
•••••••••••••••••

INTRODUCTION

In 1985 my husband learned from a routine health exam that he had high cholesterol. His cholesterol level of 258 milligrams per deciliter put him in the high-risk category for heart disease. Attached to his test results was a recommended diet, which was supposed to lower his cholesterol level.

After reading the dietary recommendations, I was doubtful they would do him much good because he was already eating a healthy diet. He never ate bacon, rarely ate eggs, butter, or liver, drank only skim milk, and ate red meat once or twice a week. After a year of following the recommended dietary restrictions, his cholesterol level fell only a few points to 243 mg/dl. He was still in the high-risk category.

It became clear to me that restricting Rick's dietary cholesterol was not enough. We had to look for the hidden dietary offenders. His diet was basically healthy, but he would not give up his cookies and desserts. He could turn away from prime ribs, but a chocolate chip cookie was too tempting. Switching from butter to margarine and shortening did little to change his cholesterol level. He had to reduce not only the cholesterol he ate but also the saturated fats. Since his favorite desserts and cookies were loaded with saturated fats, I had to invent substitutions that would satisfy his sweet tooth, taste rich, and yet be healthy and low in fat.

This assignment was made even harder because everything I cooked had to be appealing not only to the adults in the house, but to the children as well. I realized the importance of this undertaking since I knew both my husband's and my children's lives were at stake. Heart disease can be inherited, and both of my children have slightly elevated cholesterol levels. This was a life work of the most important kind.

1

Let Them Eat Cake
• • • • • • • • • • • • • • • •

After years of research and experimenting, I have compiled this collection of desserts and sweets. These recipes have received the seal of approval from taste testers of all ages. Your family will love the taste, and you will know they are eating healthier foods and perhaps extending their lives.

I have found that cookies and desserts are the hardest things to stop eating, and they often have more cholesterol and saturated fat than red meat. Butter, cream, and eggs can be harmful to someone with coronary heart disease. When you want something sweet and creamy to eat, however, it seems nothing else will suffice. It was because of this almost universal urge that I decided to direct my energies toward inventing desserts that were healthier and yet delicious. I knew people would not stop cheating. So why not give them something that would satisfy them and not compromise their health?

After a year of eating my healthier desserts and following the general recommendations for lowering cholesterol, my husband's cholesterol level came down to 193 mg/dl with a good total cholesterol to HDL ratio. His cholesterol level has stayed below the recommended level of 200 mg/dl for more than five years. As a result, his risk of a premature heart attack has been reduced by about 50 percent! All of this was achieved without giving up the desserts he loves and without medication. With a little creativity, many of the richest and fat-saturated desserts can be transformed into delicious, healthy, and low-fat desserts.

Since more than half of all adults and as many as 25 percent of all children have elevated cholesterol levels, it is important that we start eating to live longer and healthier lives.[1] It can be easier than you think. With this book, you will not feel deprived, nor will you spend hours cooking or shopping in a health-food store. This book offers you a practical and easy guide for making delicious desserts, cookies, cakes, pies, and muffins that are low in cholesterol, saturated fats and sugar. They will satisfy that sweet tooth urge when it hits. Bon appetit!

CHOLESTEROL, FAT, AND HEART DISEASE

Chances are 20 years ago you never heard of the word cholesterol. Now you hear about it almost daily, and it has developed a sinister connotation. However, cholesterol is essential to life. This fatlike substance is produced naturally by your body's cells and liver. It is used to build cell walls, make hormones, and aid in digestion. Eating large amounts of animal fats and saturated fats, though, may lead to dangerously high levels of cholesterol in the blood. Most Americans need to reduce the dietary cholesterol and saturated fat they eat. We do not need to eat cholesterol to live. The liver produces enough cholesterol to take care of our needs.

'GOOD' VERSUS 'BAD'

There has been a lot of talk about "good" and "bad" cholesterol. Cholesterol becomes harmful depending on the way it travels through the bloodstream. Lipoproteins are a fat-protein substance that act as the carrier particles of cholesterol. Low-density lipoproteins (LDLs) are called bad cholesterol because an excess of cholesterol carried by them can lead to deposits in your arteries, narrowing them and thus increasing your risk of heart attack or stroke. High-density lipoproteins (HDLs) are considered the good or healthy cholesterol carriers because they can help prevent heart disease by acting like biological sponges. HDLs soak up the cholesterol in the bloodstream not needed by the body's cells and carry it back to the liver for removal from the body.[2] If you have trouble remembering which cholesterol is good or bad, think of the "H" in HDL as an abbreviation for healthy. This should help you remember that HDL is the healthy cholesterol and LDL is the bad cholesterol.

The latest federal guidelines recommend that an adult over age 30 should have a total blood cholesterol level at or below 200 milligrams per tenth of a liter of blood (200 mg/dl). Ideally, if you are under 30, your serum cholesterol level should be under 180 mg/dl. A cholesterol level of 200 to 239 mg/dl puts you in a borderline high-risk category. A value above 240 mg/dl puts you in a high-risk category. If you have an elevated blood cholesterol level, every 1 percent decrease in blood cholesterol can lead to at least a 2 percent decrease in heart attack risk.[3] This is the most important two-for-one deal you will ever experience.

The ratio of LDL to HDL is just as important as the total serum cholesterol count. The National Heart, Lung, and Blood Institute recommends aiming for an LDL of 130 or lower and an HDL above 40.[4] For a desirable ratio, your total cholesterol divided by your HDL cholesterol should not be greater than 4.5.[5] For example, if your total cholesterol is 220 and your HDL level is 35, your HDL is too low (220 divided by 35 = 6.29). This number indicates that your total cholesterol is too high and your HDLs are too low. Some doctors believe a ratio of 3.5 or lower is ideal.

We should all try to achieve higher HDL and lower LDL levels. LDLs can be reduced dramatically by dietary restrictions. HDLs, on the other hand, are raised most effectively by increased exercise. Therefore, daily exercise and cautious use of fats seems to be the healthiest way to live.

Many doctors believe high levels of HDL and low levels of LDL play a vital role in preventing heart disease. To achieve these levels, controlling your intake of dietary cholesterol alone is not enough. You have to decrease the amount of saturated fat you eat as well. These fats increase the amount of cholesterol carried in the bloodstream, especially the LDL cholesterol.

HIDDEN DIETARY OFFENDERS

Saturated fats are usually solid at room temperature and most often come from animal by-products. There are three exceptions to remember, though. Palm oil, palm kernel oil, and coconut oil are highly saturated—even more so than lard. Used extensively by commercial bakers, the inexpensive price and long shelf life of these oils make them appealing for commercial products. The effect of saturated fat on blood cholesterol, however, is about three times worse than that of any cholesterol you might eat.[6] So the consumption of saturated fats should be reduced at all costs.

Another dietary offender is hydrogenated fat. Hydrogen gas is forced into liquid vegetable oil to make it more solid at room temperature. This process takes a relatively good dietary fat and turns into a partially saturated fat. Hydrogenated fat is found in many commercial products.

Polyunsaturated fats usually come from vegetable products and should be used to replace saturated fats. Polyunsaturated fats such as corn oil, sunflower oil, safflower oil, and soybean oil have only a 9 to 17 percent saturated fat content. Cottonseed oil has more saturated fat than other polyunsaturated fats.

The latest research indicates using monounsaturated fats such as olive oil, canola oil, or peanut oil in place of other fats may be beneficial in lowering LDL (bad) cholesterol without reducing HDL (healthy) cholesterol levels. Even so, the total fat consumption of the typical American should be reduced.

Most people believe if they avoid red meat, eggs, butter, and cream, they will lower their blood cholesterol level. However, many people do not realize that foods that are cholesterol free are not necessarily worry free. Baked products made with saturated and hydrogenated fats are very dangerous to someone with a cholesterol problem. Cookies, crackers, pies, cakes, muffins, and chocolates bought in the grocery store often contain palm oil, coconut oil, or hydrogenated fats.

CALCULATING FAT CONTENT

What should a person concerned about cholesterol do? It is recommended that you reduce your fat consumption to 25 to 30 percent of your total daily calories. There is a simple calculation you can use when buying packaged food to see what percentage of its calories comes from fat. It will require that you do some label reading, though. Soon most packaged foods will be required to carry nutritional labels. Many already do and list the fat, cholesterol, and calorie content of the item for you. Fat is measured in grams on package labels. There are nine calories to each gram of fat. The formula for calculating how many calories come from fat starts with reading the nutritional labels.

1. Find the number of grams of fat per serving and multiply that by 9.
2. Divide that answer by the number of calories per serving.
3. Multiply the answer by 100 (or move the decimal point two places to the right) and you have the percentage of fat in each serving.

In other words:

$$\frac{(9 \times \text{fat grams per serving}) \times 100}{\text{Total calories per serving}} = \begin{array}{l} \text{Percentage of} \\ \text{calories from fat} \end{array}$$

Do not lose heart; it is not as difficult as it may seem. Here is an example of the equation using a low-fat yogurt. The yogurt has 2 grams of fat and 190 calories per serving. Two grams of fat multiplied by nine equals eighteen calories that come from fat. Eighteen fat calories divided by 190 total calories equals .09 or 9 percent. Nine percent is well below the recommended fat intake of 25 percent and therefore acceptable. Moreover, this means that 91 percent of the calories in the yogurt comes from something other than fat, and, hopefully, something more nutritious.

You will be shocked by your calculations. Packaged potato chips and popcorn often derive more than 50 percent of their calories from fat. Regular yogurt and cottage cheese are not much better. Even 2 percent milk derives 38 percent of its calories from fat. A note of caution: Do not be fooled by labels proclaiming the product to be "light." This does not always refer to the amount of fat used and does not tell you anything about the kind of fat used. Also, beware of the label "cholesterol free." Most potato chips are and always have been cholesterol free but derive up to 60 percent of their calories from fat. Always read the nutritional label before making a decision.

HEALTHY SUBSTITUTIONS

Along with reading labels, I have changed some of my cooking habits. I do not bake with a lot of margarine, butter, or shortening anymore. Margarine is made up of 80 percent polyunsaturated fat, which has often been hydrogenated and therefore turned into partially saturated fat. If you choose to use margarine, select the softer or less hydrogenated version.

Butter is made up of 80 percent to 82 percent saturated fat and contains cholesterol. Vegetable shortening may not have cholesterol, but it consists of 98 percent fat with 3 grams of saturated fat and 3 grams of polyunsaturated fat. I have substituted vegetable oils low in saturated fat for these fats. In most cases, I have been able to reduce the amount of oil used, therefore reducing the amount of fat and calories in the recipe. And I have been careful to do this without jeopardizing the rich and delicious taste of each dessert. My desserts do not have the light, airy, and spongy taste common with most low-fat and low-cholesterol desserts.

When buying vegetable oils, look for a high polyunsaturated-to-saturated-fat ratio. A ratio of 2-to-1 or greater is desirable.[7] Monounsaturated oils are even better. Research shows that while polyunsaturated oils lower both the good and bad cholesterol, monounsaturated oils, such as olive, peanut, or canola oil, lower only LDL.[8]

In most of my baking, I use only polyunsaturated or monounsaturated oils, and as little of these as possible. If a butter taste is desired, I use a natural dehydrated butter like Butter Buds®. It is all natural and filled with a buttery taste without any of the fat.

When a cake recipe calls for an egg, substituting two egg whites usually does not affect the taste. A side benefit to all these substitutions is there are fewer calories in my baked goods.

Many dessert recipes call for cream. Depending on the taste I want, I substitute skim milk, nonfat yogurt, or low-fat cottage cheese. These fat-reduced products can often replace cream cheese as well. Most supermarkets now carry low-fat and nonfat sour creams and ricotta cheeses. I have been able to take sinfully rich cheesecake recipes and modify them into delicious cheesecakes that will not compromise my family's health.

Most low-cholesterol diets also recommend increasing fiber consumption. Foods containing water-soluble fibers are very effective in lowering blood cholesterol levels. Oat bran contains a higher amount of soluble fiber than most grains. Some studies have concluded that consuming large amounts of oat bran can slow down cholesterol synthesis in the liver, regulate blood sugar, increase HDL levels, and stimulate the removal of LDLs from the bloodstream.[9] For this reason, I have included oat bran and other fiber-rich foods, such as rolled oats, wheat germ, and whole-wheat flour in many of my recipes. In most cases, using a more fiber-rich flour will not alter the taste of the recipe.

Eating more fruit is an enjoyable way to lower cholesterol. Fresh fruit contains fiber and pectin, which have been proved to help lower blood cholesterol levels. Fruit's natural sweetness can also enhance the flavor of many desserts.

About 20 percent to 25 percent of the average American's daily caloric consumption comes from sugar, which does not provide any of the nutrients essential to life.[10] Sugar, whether white, brown, or raw, is nutritionally "empty," as is honey and fructose. Molasses is the only sweetener that provides the body with a trace of nutrients, including iron. Furthermore, for many people, a high-sugar diet may result in elevated levels of blood fats called triglycerides. I have found that by combining different sweeteners, I have been able to obtain a desirable sweet taste in my baked goods while using less sugar.

We have now arrived at the point where it is time to stop reading about healthier desserts and start making them. Armed with the information provided in this book, you can stop depriving yourself of desserts. You will not be able to change your eating habits permanently if you completely avoid the foods you love. You can learn to modify these foods into heart-healthy feasts. These desserts are about to become "fare for your heart."

RECIPE NOTES

If you are trying to lower your cholesterol, you may find yourself baking more than you ever have. Commercially baked goods are usually full of saturated fats and therefore should be avoided. This book explains how to bake healthier desserts without spending hours in the kitchen or hours shopping in a health-food store. You will learn how to bake more of your favorite desserts while using less fat and cholesterol. Just remember that all desserts should be eaten in moderation.

FLOURS

All-purpose flour is the least expensive to buy, but it is also the least nutritious. This white flour comes from the heart of the wheat kernel and has been stripped of most of its vitamins, minerals, and fiber. When buying this flour, look for the enriched, unbleached variety.

Stone-ground whole-wheat flour, on the other hand, is a good source of protein, fiber, calcium, phosphorus, potassium, and other minerals. It is a coarser flour, though, and not as light as white flour. For this reason, I have used a mixture of these flours in most of my recipes. If you can find whole-wheat pastry flour, it will make a lighter cake and a flakier pie crust than regular whole-wheat flour. You may need to add one to two tablespoons of pastry flour for every cup of regular flour called for in the recipe. Mixing all-purpose flour and whole-wheat flour improves the nutrition value and increases the fiber content of the baked goods.

Stone-ground whole-wheat flour does not have as long a shelf life as all-purpose flour. Since it becomes rancid in a few months, it should be stored in the refrigerator or freezer. Putting a bay leaf in any flour stored outside the refrigerator will discourage insect invasions.

Grains such as barley, oats, rye, and buckwheat ground into flour can be used in baking for a variety of tastes. Be careful, though, since many of these flours do not contain enough gluten to make raised yeast breads. They need to be mixed with a gluten-containing wheat flour. These flours also need to be refrigerated.

I usually sift all flours before using them because they become packed down during storage. If you do not sift your flour, you may be adding too much to your recipe. Sifting the flour and baking powder or soda together will ensure those ingredients are mixed well.

Many of the recipes in this book call for the addition of quick rolled oats or oat bran. Some of the latest research indicates that eating one bowl of regular oatmeal and two oat bran muffins may lead to a 25 percent decrease in serum cholesterol levels.[11]

I make my own oat flour by whirling rolled oats in the food processor for 60 seconds. I use this oat flour in some of my cookies and quick breads. It gives the baked product more texture and a nuttier flavor. In addition, oats contain a natural preservative that gives foods a longer shelf life. Oat flour, however, does not contain gluten and must be mixed with a gluten-containing flour in order to rise.

NATURAL SWEETENERS

In most of my baked goods, I combine a number of all-natural liquid sweeteners with great success. When using sugar, I usually use the brown variety because it is less processed. Keep in mind, though, that most sweeteners do not provide any of our daily essential nutrients. Molasses is the exception because it contains a small amount of nutrients and iron. I have found I can reduce the amount of sweeteners by one-fourth or more without missing them.

When using natural liquid sweeteners such as honey, molasses, and maple syrup, you must adjust the recipe. If you add one cup of liquid sweetener, reduce the other liquid in the recipe by one-quarter cup. If less than a cup of liquid sweetener is used, convert the recipe proportionately.

Honey is sweeter than sugar, so less honey is required. The following table will help you adjust your recipes. Replace each cup of granulated sugar with:

- 1/2 to 3/4 cup of honey
- 2/3 to 3/4 cup of maple syrup
- 3/4 cup of molasses
- 1/2 cup honey plus 1/4 cup molasses
- 1/2 cup honey plus 1/4 cup of maple syrup[12]

When cooking with molasses, you have to adjust for the different chemical reactions that occur between molasses and baking soda and baking powder. For each cup of molasses or molasses combined with honey, you must add 1/2 teaspoon baking soda and decrease the baking powder in the recipe by two teaspoons.[13] If you are using less than a cup of molasses, convert the recipe proportionately. I have found that baking soda has a stronger taste than baking powder, so your adjustments may take some experimenting.

Natural liquid sweeteners help to make chewy rather than crisp cookies. An added benefit is that since liquid sweeteners attract moisture, they keep baked goods from becoming stale quickly. Do not use raw (uncooked) honey with infants. Their immature digestive systems do not handle it properly.

OILS

All fats and oils are composed of varying combinations of fatty acids. Depending on the composition of these molecules, the fats or oils are termed saturated, monounsaturated, or polyunsaturated.

Saturated fats are usually solid at room temperature and generally come from animal by-products. These fats should be avoided or used with great care because they can raise serum (blood) cholesterol levels and clog arteries. It might be helpful to remember that if the fat is solid at room temperature, it may end up the same way in your arteries. The tropical oils (palm oil, palm kernel oil, and coconut oil) are also highly saturated and should not be eaten. While most of us would never buy these oils, they are used in many commercial desserts and cookies.

Polyunsaturated fats and oils come from vegetable by-products. Replacing the saturated fats you eat with these oils may help reduce your total blood cholesterol. The most common polyunsaturated oils used are corn oil, safflower oil, soybean oil, and sunflower oil. Cottonseed oil is polyunsaturated but has more saturated fat than the others. Most polyunsaturated oils contain saturated, polyunsaturated, and monounsaturated fat. Choose oils with a high polyunsaturated-to-saturated-fat ratio. A ratio of 2-to-1 or better is the healthiest.

Monounsaturated fats are the healthiest fats to eat because they lower the level of the bad cholesterol, LDL, without lowering the healthy cholesterol, HDL. Avocado, olive, peanut, and canola oil are the most common monounsaturated oils.

Replacing your butter with margarine is not the answer. Margarine has been hydrogenated and, therefore, partly saturated so it will remain solid at room temperature. However, margarine does not contain cholesterol and therefore is less damaging than butter. Use as little margarine as possible and look for the softer, less hydrogenated varieties. The nutritional labels on most margarines and oils will tell you how much saturated and polyunsaturated fat they contain. Remember to limit the amount of all fats in your diet to less than 30 percent of your daily calories.

Most of my recipes call for a vegetable oil low in saturated fat, such as safflower oil, canola oil, or a light-tasting peanut oil instead of shortening, margarine, or butter. Shortening and margarine are filled with saturated fats, and butter is not only highly saturated but full of cholesterol. Polyunsaturated and monunsaturated oils, on the other hand, have been found effective in lowering blood cholesterol in many cases. More important, the monounsaturated oils like olive oil, canola oil, and peanut oil have been shown to lower the levels of harmful LDLs without lowering the healthy HDLs. Unlike some of the other monounsaturates, canola oil or a light-tasting peanut oil can be used for baking. You may be able to find a light-tasting olive oil that will not have too heavy an olive taste for your baking.

I have found when I cook with oil, I am able to reduce the amount of fat by at least 25 percent. I can usually cut the fat even more when I combine oils with natural liquid sweeteners. In this way, I can reduce the fat and calories in my baked products. This results in healthier baked goods.

When baking with oils, you will get chewier cookies and crunchier pie crusts. Flaky pie crusts require saturated fats. A combination of oil and butter, margarine or shortening results in a flakier crust, albeit less healthy. Vegetable oil sprays can often be used to grease cookie sheets and pie plates.

EGGS

As previously noted, when a recipe calls for an egg, I usually substitute two egg whites. All my recipes call for the use of egg whites from large eggs. When a recipe calls for six eggs, you do not have to use 12 egg whites. Try using eight egg whites and adding a little more of whatever other liquid is in the recipe.

Egg whites require special attention when they are to be beaten. Be sure that your egg beaters are clean and dry and that the egg whites are at room temperature before beating them. If they are not, the egg whites will not become light and fluffy after being beaten. Grease of any kind on the bowl or utensils will also ruin the results.

SODIUM REDUCTION

At this point, I think it is important to mention how to reduce sodium consumption for those people on a low-fat and low-sodium diet. Many doctors recommend using 1,100 milligrams of sodium or less a day—about half of what most of us use.[14] To achieve this healthy level, you need to cut down or eliminate the salt you add to your dishes and to read labels for ingredients containing hidden sodium.

The recipes in this book use reduced amounts of salt or no salt at all. Baking soda and baking powder are the only other high-sodium-containing ingredients consistently called for in many of the recipes. In most cases, though, the individual serving of each item is not high in sodium.

Let Them Eat Cake
● ● ● ● ● ● ● ● ● ● ● ● ● ● ● ● ●

References

1. "Heart Health," *Newsweek,* Feb 13, 1989, p. S-7
2. Greater Cincinnati Nutrition Council, "Food for Thought," Cincinnati, OH: Jan/Feb, 1988, pp. 1-4
3. Brand, David: "Searching for Life's Elixir," *Time,* Dec 12, 1988, pp. 62-66
4. Ibid, p. 64
5. Greater Cincinnati Nutrition Council: op. cit., p. 2
6. Ibid., p. 2
7. Ibid., p. 3
8. Mazzeo-Caputo, Stephanie: "Heart Healthy Eating, *Newsweek,* Feb 13, 1989, p. S-12
9. Anderson, James, M.D: "Hypocholesterolemic Effects of Oat or Bean Products," *First International Congress on Vegetarian Nutrition,* Washington, DC, Mar 16, 1987
10. Brody, Jane: *Good Food Book,* New York: Bantam Books, 1987, p. 13
11. Anderson, James, M.D.: op cit.
12. Goldbeck, Nikki, Goldbeck, David: *American Wholefoods Cuisine,* New York: New American Library, 1984, p. 367
13. Ibid, p. 367
14. Brody, Jane: op cit., p. 15

ABOUT CAKES

This section of the book was most fun to do. I collected the richest and most decadent cake recipes I could find and transformed them into delicious and healthier cakes. You will probably find some of your favorite cake recipes in here. They will taste as delicious and sinful as the original, but they will have less than half the fat, almost none of the cholesterol, fewer calories, and more fiber than the original version.

There are cake recipes for all occasions and tastes in this book. Some of the cakes are very healthy, even though no one will suspect that, and some are less so. Look through this chapter and find the recipes that tempt your taste buds—without damaging your heart.

Go ahead and serve my cheesecake for dinner, but don't tell anyone it isn't sinfully rich until after it is eaten. Everyone will be surprised at how good these desserts are. You no longer have to feel deprived or guilty. Once you have tried these recipes, you will throw out your old ones!

APPLESAUCE SPICE CAKE

This delicious cake has no cholesterol and only a trace of saturated fat. It is actually brimming with healthy ingredients—but no one will ever suspect that!

1 cup sifted all-purpose unbleached flour
1 cup sifted stone-ground whole-wheat flour
1 1/2 teaspoons baking powder
1 1/2 teaspoons baking soda
1/2 cup oat bran
1 teaspoon ground cinnamon
1/2 teaspoon ground ginger
1/4 teaspoon freshly ground nutmeg
1/2 teaspoon ground cloves
1/2 teaspoon salt
1/4 cup granulated sugar (optional, depending
*   on desired sweetness)*
3/4 cup lightly packed brown sugar
4 egg whites at room temperature
1/4 cup canola oil, low-in-saturated-fat vegetable oil,
*   or light-tasting peanut oil*
2/3 cup apple juice
1 teaspoon vanilla extract
1/4 cup honey
2 cups unsweetened applesauce
1 cup raisins (optional)

Preheat oven to 350°. Grease and flour a 12-cup Bundt™ or tube pan. Sift both flours, baking powder, and baking soda into a large bowl. Mix in the oat bran, cinnamon, ginger, nutmeg, cloves, salt, and both sugars until there are no lumps. In another bowl, beat the egg whites until soft peaks form. Beat in the oil, apple juice, vanilla, honey, and applesauce. Stir half of the applesauce mixture into the flour mixture. Beat in the rest of the applesauce mixture. Beat on high for one minute until everything is mixed well together. Mix in the raisins. Pour into the prepared pan and bake in a preheated oven for 50 to 60 minutes or until a cake tester comes out clean. Let the cake cool and remove from the pan. Cover with lemon glaze.

Serves 14.

Nutrition Values

Calories 234	Dietary fiber 2.8 gm
Carbohydrate 48 gm	Percentage of calories from
Cholesterol 0	Protein 6%
Sodium 222 mg	Carbohydrate 78%
Protein 4 gm	Fat 16%
Total fat 4 gm	Exchanges
Polyunsaturated fat, 1.5 gm	1 fruit
Monounsaturated fat, 2 gm	1 starch/bread
Saturated fat, 0.76 gm	1 fat

LEMON GLAZE

*1/2 cup powdered sugar (Add more powdered sugar
     if you prefer a thicker glaze.)
2 to 4 teaspoons fresh lemon juice (Add more lemon
     juice to make the glaze thinner.)*

In a small mixing bowl, combine the powdered sugar and lemon juice. Mix until smooth. Drizzle the glaze over the cake.

Nutrition values

Calories 14	All others 0
Carbohydrate 4	Exchanges Free

APPLE TOPPED CAKE

This is a very popular dessert in my house. It is easy to make and filled with delicious, healthy ingredients.

> *3/4 cup sifted all-purpose unbleached flour*
> *3/4 cup sifted stone-ground whole-wheat flour*
> *1 teaspoon baking powder*
> *1/4 cup honey*
> *1/2 cup lightly packed brown sugar*
> *1/4 cup vegetable, canola, or light-tasting peanut oil*
> *4 large egg whites*
> *1 tablespoon nonfat plain yogurt*
> *5 peeled, cored, and thinly sliced apples*

Topping
> *Bring to a boil:*
> *2 tablespoons vegetable, canola, or light-tasting peanut oil*
> *1/4 cup granulated or brown sugar*
> *1 teaspoon cinnamon*
> *1 teaspoon natural dehydrated butter (optional)*

Preheat the oven to 425°. Grease a 9- x 13-inch baking pan. Sift both flours and the baking powder together in a medium-sized bowl. Beat the honey, 1/2 cup brown sugar, vegetable oil, egg whites, and nonfat yogurt together. Pour this into the flour mixture and stir well. Pour the dough into the prepared pan and smooth is out evenly. Lightly press the apples into the dough in straight lines. Bake for 10 minutes at 425°. Remove the cake from the oven. Drizzle the topping over the top of the apples. Return the cake to the oven and bake at 375° for 15 to 20 minutes or until cake tester comes out clean.

Serves 12.

Nutrition Values

Calories 222
Carbohydrates 39 gm
Cholesterol 0
Sodium 51 mg
Protein 3 gm
Total fat 7 gm
Polyunsaturated fat 3 gm
Monounsaturated fat 3 gm
Saturated fat 1 gm

Dietary fiber 2 gm
Percentage of calories from
  Protein 5%
  Carbohydrate 67%
  Fat 28%
Exchanges
  1 bread
  1/2 fruit
  1 1/2 fat

APRICOT SPICE CAKE

The slight hint of apricot enhances the delicious mixture of subtle tastes found in this cake. If you would prefer a lighter, whiter cake, leave out the whole-wheat flour and oat bran and increase the sifted all-purpose flour to 2 cups.

1/2 to 3/4 cup dried apricots
1 teaspoon granulated sugar
1/2 cup orange juice
3 large egg whites at room temperature
1/3 cup vegetable, canola, or light-tasting peanut oil
1/2 cup lightly packed brown sugar
1 tablespoon granulated sugar
1 tablespoon honey
1 teaspoon vanilla extract
1 cup sifted unbleached all-purpose flour
1/2 cup sifted stone-ground whole-wheat flour

1 teaspoon baking powder
1 teaspoon baking soda
1/2 cup oat bran
1 teaspoon ground cinnamon
1/4 teaspoon freshly ground nutmeg
1/2 teaspoon ground cloves
1/4 teaspoon ground ginger
1 cup skim buttermilk

Preheat oven to 350°. Grease and flour a 12-cup Bundt™ pan or tube pan. Using a small bowl, soak the apricots and 1 teaspoon sugar in the orange juice for 1 hour. Drain and save the juice. Puree the apricots in a food processor with 3 tablespoons of the drained orange juice. Set aside. In a large bowl, beat the egg whites until frothy. Beat in the vegetable oil, both sugars, honey, and vanilla. Set aside. Sift both flours, baking powder, and baking soda together. Stir in the oat bran and spices. Stir the dry ingredients into the bowl of liquid ingredients alternating with the buttermilk. Stir in the apricot puree. Pour into a prepared Bundt™ pan. Bake for 50 to 55 minutes or until a cake tester comes out clean. Let cool, remove from pan, and cover with glaze.
Serves 14.

GLAZE

1/4 cup brown sugar
3 tablespoons orange juice
1 tablespoon margarine

While stirring, bring the ingredients to a boil. Continue to boil slowly for 5 minutes, stirring occasionally. Let cool and drizzle the glaze over the cake.

Nutrition Values

Calories 190
Carbohydrates 32 gm
Cholesterol 0.2 mg
Sodium 118 mg
Protein 3.3 gm
Total fat 6.4 gm
Polyunsaturated fat 2 gm
Monounsaturated fat 3 gm
Saturated fat 1.1 gm

Total dietary fiber 1.3 gm
Percent of calories from
  Protein 7%
  Carbohydrates 64%
  Fat 29%
Exchanges
  1 Bread
  1 Fat
  1/2 Fruit

BANANA APPLE CAKE

This is a quick and delicious way to use up your apple harvest. The banana keeps the cake moist and gives it a delicious taste.

6 to 8 large assorted apples, peeled, cored, and thinly sliced
1/3 to 1/2 cup brown sugar
1 1/2 teaspoons ground cinnamon
2 cups sifted, unbleached all-purpose flour
1 teaspoon baking powder
1/2 teaspoon baking soda
2 large egg whites
3 tablespoons canola oil, low-in-saturated-fat vegetable oil,
    or light-tasting peanut oil
1 tablespoon Butter Buds® (all-natural dehydrated butter)
1/2 cup nonfat milk
1/4 cup nonfat plain yogurt
1/4 cup honey

Let Them Eat Cake
• • • • • • • • • • • • • • • •

4 tablespoons granulated sugar
1 small overripe banana, mashed
Vegetable cooking spray

Preheat oven to 375°. Spray a 9- x 13-inch pan with vegetable cooking spray. Mix the apples, sugar, and cinnamon together in a bowl. Set aside. Sift the flour, baking powder, and baking soda together into a large bowl. In another bowl, beat the egg whites until light and frothy. Beat in the vegetable oil, Butter Buds®, nonfat milk, yogurt, honey, sugar, and mashed banana. Mix the liquid ingredients into the dry ingredients. Smooth the batter into the sprayed pan. Place the apple slices on top of the dough and press them into the dough. (You can make decorative rows or just dump the apples on top.) Drizzle any apple juice left in the bowl over the apples and dough. Bake at 375° for 10 minutes and 350° for 30 to 35 minutes more or until cooked through. Serve warm or cool. Refrigerate if not eaten in a day.
Serves 12.

Nutrition Values

Calories 240
Carbohydrates 50 gm
Cholesterol 0.2 mg
Sodium 84 mg
Protein 3 gm
Total fat 4 gm
Polyunsaturated fat 1.3 gm
Monounsaturated fat 1.6 gm
Saturated fat 0.7 gm
Dietary fiber 2.63 gm

Percentage of calories from
  Protein 5%
  Carbohydrate 81%
  Fat 14%

Exchanges:
  1 bread
  1 fruit
  1 fat

BANANA CAKE

This cake was inspired by a delicious, rich gourmet recipe that I could no longer make because of the high cholesterol and fat content. You, too, can take very rich recipes found in gourmet books and magazines and transform them into delicious, healthier recipes.

1 cup sifted whole-wheat flour
1 cup sifted unbleached enriched all-purpose flour
1 teaspoon baking powder
1 teaspoon baking soda
1/4 teaspoon salt (optional)
1 cup mashed ripe bananas (about 2 medium-sized)
1/2 cup honey
1/2 cup granulated sugar
1 to 2 teaspoons lemon juice
1/2 cup canola oil, low-in-saturated-fat vegetable oil,
    or light-tasting peanut oil
1/4 cup banana liqueur
2 teaspoons vanilla extract
1/4 cup skim milk
6 large egg whites at room temperature
1/2 teaspoon cream of tartar

Preheat oven to 350°. Grease and flour a 12-cup tube pan that has a removable bottom. Sift together both flours, baking powder, baking soda, and salt into a large bowl. Mash the bananas in a medium-size bowl. Beat in the honey, sugar, lemon juice, vegetable oil, banana liqueur, and vanilla until well mixed. Stir the bowl of liquid ingredients into the bowl of dry ingredients. Beat in the milk for about one minute. In another bowl, combine the egg whites and cream of tartar. Beat the egg whites with clean, dry beaters until stiff but not dry. Fold half of the egg whites at a time into the batter. Pour batter into prepared pan. Bake in a preheated oven for 50 minutes or until cake tester comes out clean. Let cool and remove cake from pan. Spread Banana Cake Frosting on the top of the cake.

Serves 14.

BANANA CAKE FROSTING

1/2 cup brown sugar
1 large egg white
1/2 teaspoon vanilla extract
1/2 teaspoon maple flavor (optional)

With an electric beater carefully beat sugar and egg white in the top of a double boiler over boiling water until peaks form— about 3 minutes. Add vanilla and maple flavor and beat one more minute. Remove from heat and frost the top of the cake.

Nutrition Values

Calories 259
Carbohydrates 43 gm
Cholesterol 0 mg
Sodium 154 mg
Protein 4 gm
Total fat 8 gm
Polyunsaturated fat 2.6 gm
Monounsaturated fat 3.6 gm
Saturated fat 1.4 gm
Dietary fiber 1.6 gm

Percentage of calories from
    Protein 6%
    Carbohydrate 64%
    Fat 27%
Exchanges
    1 bread
    1 1/2 fat
    1/2 fruit
    1/2 meat

BANANA STRAWBERRY CAKE

Here is a dessert that will delight the young and the old.

1/2 cup granulated sugar
1/2 cup mild-tasting honey
1/2 cup vegetable, canola, or light-tasting peanut oil
1/2 cup mashed ripe banana (1 large banana)
1/2 cup nonfat plain yogurt
1/2 cup skim milk
1 teaspoon vanilla extract
3 cups sifted unbleached all-purpose flour
1 teaspoon baking powder
3/4 teaspoon baking soda
7 large egg whites at room temperature
*1/2 cup strawberry preserves (try the juice-sweetened
  or reduced sugar variety)*

Preheat oven to 350°. Grease and flour a 12-cup tube or Bundt™ cake pan. Beat together the sugar, honey, vegetable oil, and mashed banana. Set aside. Mix the yogurt, milk, and vanilla together in a small bowl. Set aside. Sift the flour, baking powder, and baking soda together. Stir the dry ingredients into the banana mixture alternating with the yogurt mixture. Beat for 60 seconds.

Wash and dry the beaters. Beat the egg whites until very frothy. Stir into the batter. Remove 2 cups of the batter. Mix this with the strawberry preserves. Spoon half of the original batter into the tube pan. Spoon all of the strawberry batter over this. Cover with the remaining batter. Bake for 60 to 70 minutes or until a cake tester comes out clean. Cool the cake in the pan for 10 minutes. Remove the cake from the pan and let cool completely before serving.

Serves 14.

Nutrition Values

Calories 254
Carbohydrates 42 gm
Cholesterol 0.2 mg
Sodium 117 mg
Protein 5 gm
Total fat 8 gm
Polyunsaturated fat 2.6 gm
Monounsaturated fat 3.6 gm
Saturated fat 1.3 gm
Dietary fiber 0.8 gm

Percentage of calories from
  Protein 7%
  Carbohydrate 65%
  Fat 28%
Exchanges
  1 1/2 bread
  1 1/2 fat
  1/2 fruit
  1/2 meat

BASIC YELLOW CAKE

This cake is perfect for those times when you need a plain, basic cake recipe. I use this recipe to make the children's birthday cupcakes. It may not have the nutrition of a whole-wheat or oat bran cake, but it is low in fat, has very little cholesterol, and is popular with the children.

2 1/2 cups sifted unbleached all-purpose flour
3 teaspoons baking powder
1/4 teaspoon baking soda
4 large egg whites at room temperature
1/4 teaspoon cream of tartar
3/4 cup granulated sugar
1 cup skim milk

Cakes
• • • • • • • • • • • • • • • •

1/3 cup canola oil or low-in-saturated-fat vegetable oil
1 teaspoon vanilla extract
1/4 teaspoon almond extract
1/4 cup mild-tasting honey

Preheat oven to 350°. Grease and flour two 9-inch round cake pans or 24-muffin tins. Sift the flour, baking powder, and baking soda together into a large mixing bowl. Set aside. Beat the egg whites until foamy. Add the cream of tartar and continue to beat until soft peaks form. While still beating, gradually add the sugar. Set aside. In another bowl, beat the milk, vegetable oil, vanilla, almond extract, and honey together. Pour this into the dry ingredients and beat until everything is smooth. Fold in the egg whites. Pour into the prepared pans or muffin tins. Bake the cake 25 to 30 minutes or the muffins 18 to 20 minutes. Be sure a cake tester comes out clean from the cake or muffins before removing them from the oven. Cool and frost with a standard Seven-Minute White Frosting or my Fluffy Fatless Chocolate Frosting.
Serves 12 or makes 24 cupcakes.

Nutrition Values

Calories 108
Carbohydrates 18.5 gm
Cholesterol 0
Sodium 65.5 mg
Protein 2 gm
Total fat 3 gm
Polyunsaturated fat 1 gm
Monounsaturated fat 1.4 gm
Saturated fat 0.5 gm

Dietary fiber 0.3 gm

Percentage of calories from
   Protein 7%
   Carbohydrate 68%
   Fat 25%
Exchanges:
   1 bread
   1 fat

29

BLUEBERRY STREUSEL CAKE

I love to make this cake when blueberries are fresh and abundant. My family loves to eat this at any time of the year.

> 2 1/2 cups sifted unbleached enriched all-purpose flour
> 1 teaspoon baking powder
> 3/4 teaspoon baking soda
> 1/2 cup oat bran
> 1/2 cup packed brown sugar
> 1/2 teaspoon ground nutmeg
> 1 teaspoon ground cinnamon
> 1/3 cup canola oil, low-in-saturated-fat vegetable oil,
>   or light-tasting peanut oil
> 1/4 cup + 1 tablespoon honey
> 1 cup nonfat milk
> 1 teaspoon vanilla extract
> 5 large egg whites at room temperature
> 2 tablespoons granulated sugar
> 1 pint washed and dried fresh blueberries
> vegetable cooking spray

Streusel topping

Combine the following ingredients until crumbly:

> 3/4 cup unbleached all-purpose flour
> 3/4 cup quick rolled oats
> 1/2 cup packed brown sugar
> 2 tablespoons vegetable oil
> 1 tablespoon shortening
> 2 tablespoons honey

Cakes
• • • • • • • • • • • • • • •

Preheat oven to 350°. Spray a 9- x 13-inch pan with vegetable cooking spray. Sift the flour, baking powder, and baking soda together into a large bowl. Stir in the oat bran, sugar, and spices. Set aside. Beat the oil, honey, milk, and vanilla together and stir well into the dry ingredients. Beat the egg whites until soft peaks form. Fold into the batter.

Spread the batter into the prepared pan. Sprinkle the granulated sugar over the blueberries and spread them over the batter. Sprinkle all the streusel topping over the blueberries and batter. Bake for 40 minutes or until cooked through. Let cool.

Serves 12.

Nutrition Values

Calories 380
Carbohydrates 67 gm
Cholesterol 0.3 mg
Sodium 121 mg
Protein 7 gm
Total fat 11 gm
Polyunsaturated fat 3.4 gm
Monounsaturated fat 5.0 gm
Saturated fat 2 gm

Dietary fiber 3.1 gm
Percentage of calories from
 Protein 7%
 Carbohydrate 68%
 Fat 25%

Exchanges
 2 bread
 2 fat

CARROT CAKE

Most carrot cake recipes call for lots of vegetable oil and a very thick cream cheese frosting. After making this recipe, you will never go back to the more fat-filled version.

> 1/2 cup canola oil, low-in-saturated-fat vegetable oil,
>   or light-tasting peanut oil
> 1/2 cup honey
> 1/2 cup packed brown sugar
> 2 tablespoons molasses
> 1 1/2 teaspoons ground cinnamon
> 1/2 teaspoon ground nutmeg
> 1 tablespoon grated lemon peel
> 1 teaspoon vanilla extract
> 1 cup sifted stone-ground whole-wheat flour
> 1 cup sifted all-purpose unbleached flour
> 1 1/2 teaspoons baking soda
> 1 1/2 teaspoons baking powder
> 1/2 cup oat bran
> 1/2 teaspoon salt (optional)
> 1/2 cup rolled oats
> 1 cup orange juice
> 2 cups finely grated carrots, cleaned and peeled
> 4 large egg whites at room temperature

Preheat oven to 350°. Grease and flour a 12-cup Bundt™ or tube pan. In a large bowl, mix together the vegetable oil, honey, brown sugar, and molasses until there are no lumps. Stir in the cinnamon, nutmeg, lemon peel, and vanilla. Set aside. Sift together both flours, baking soda, and baking powder into another bowl. Mix in the oat bran and salt. Put the rolled oats

Cakes

• • • • • • • • • • • • • •

into a food processor. Using the steel blade, whirl the oats for 60 seconds to make oat flour. Mix the ground oats into the bowl of flour and oat bran. Stir a third of the flour mixture into the vegetable oil mixture alternating with the orange juice. Repeat this process until all the flour and orange juice are mixed into the first bowl. Stir in the grated carrots. Beat the egg whites until soft peaks form. Fold them into the batter. Pour the batter into the prepared tube pan. Bake for 60 minutes or until a cake tester comes out clean. Remove the cake from the oven and cool 15 minutes. Turn the cake out of the pan and cool completely.

Serves 14.

CREAM CHEESE GLAZE

1 tablespoon light cream cheese
1 tablespoon vegetable oil
1/4 cup powdered sugar
1 teaspoon lemon juice

Combine all ingredients in a small saucepan and cook over medium heat. Stir until everything is dissolved. Remove from heat and cool until the glaze is thick enough to spoon over cake.

Nutrition Values

Calories 268
Carbohydrates 43 gm
Cholesterol 0.3 mg
Sodium 231 mg
Protein 5 gm
Total fat 10 gm
Polyunsaturated fat 3.1 gm
Monounsaturated fat 4.3 gm
Saturated fat 1.7 gm

Total dietary fiber 3.0 gm
Percentage of calories from
  Protein 7%
  Carbohydrate 62%
  Fat 32%
Exchanges
  1 bread
  2 fat
  1/2 fruit

CHOCOLATE ANGEL FOOD CAKE

This little bit of heaven tastes devilishly good, even though it has no cholesterol and just a trace of fat.

1 cup cake flour, sifted before measuring
1/4 cup unsweetened cocoa powder
1/3 cup granulated sugar
11 large egg whites at room temperature
1 teaspoon cream of tartar
3/4 cups granulated sugar
1 teaspoon vanilla extract
1/2 teaspoon chocolate flavor (optional)

Preheat oven to 350°. Lightly grease a 10-cup tube pan with removable bottom and dust with cocoa powder. Resift the cake flour five times with the cocoa powder and 1/3 cup granulated sugar. Using 1/4 of the egg whites at a time, whip all the whites until foamy. (See notes below about beating egg whites.) Add the cream of tartar when all 11 egg whites are foamy. Continue to whip the egg whites, adding 1/4 cup of sugar, 1 tablespoon at a time. When egg whites are stiff but not dry, whisk in the remaining 1/2 cup of sugar, 1 tablespoon at a time. Stir the vanilla extract and chocolate flavor into the beaten egg whites. Sift 1/4 of the flour mixture into the batter and fold in gently. Repeat until finished with the flour. Pour the batter into the prepared tube pan. Gently move a knife through the batter to remove air pockets. Bake in the preheated oven for 45 minutes. Invert pan and let cool for 1 1/2 hours. Remove from pan and drizzle with vanilla glaze.

Beating egg whites

Use a deep glass bowl and a thin wire wisk. Do not use an aluminum or plastic bowl. Since this recipe calls for cream of tartar, do not use a copper bowl. The egg whites should be about 75° in temperature and should contain no egg yolk. Grease of any kind on the bowl or utensils will ruin the results. Beat about 150 strokes a minute and increase the pace as the egg whites pass the foamy stage. Do not stop beating once you start. You can use an electric beater instead, but the egg whites will not be as fluffy.

Serves 14.

VANILLA GLAZE

1/2 cup powdered sugar
1/4 teaspoon vanilla extract
2 to 3 teaspoons water

Stir all ingredients together until smooth. Pour over cake.

Nutrition Values

Calories 115
Carbohydrates 26 gm
Cholesterol 0
Sodium 45 mg
Protein 4 gm
Total fat 0.3 gm
Polyunsaturated fat 0
Monounsaturated fat 0
Saturated fat 0.1 gm

Total dietary fiber 0.2 gm
Percentage of calories from
    Protein 12%
    Carbohydrate 86%
    Fat 2%

Exchanges
    1/2 bread
    1/2 meat

CHOCOLATE DIVINE CAKE

Even though there is very little cholesterol and saturated fat in this cake, it is divinely moist and delicious. No one will ever guess that this cake is not sinfully rich. Yes, there is life after chocolate!

1 cup sifted all-purpose unbleached flour
3/4 cup sifted stone-ground whole-wheat flour
1/2 cup unsweetened cocoa powder
1 1/2 teaspoons baking soda
1/4 teaspoon salt (optional)
1 cup granulated sugar
1/4 cup + 2 tablespoons lightly packed brown sugar
1 medium baking potato (4 ounces), peeled and quartered
1 pint nonfat plain yogurt or nonfat sour cream
2 tablespoons mild honey
1/4 teaspoon vanilla extract
1/4 teaspoon chocolate flavor (optional)
*1/3 cup canola oil, low-in-saturated-fat vegetable oil, or
    light-tasting peanut oil*
3 large egg whites at room temperature

Preheat oven to 350°. Grease a 12-cup Bundt™ pan and dust with unsweetened cocoa powder. Over a large bowl, sift both flours, cocoa powder, baking soda, and salt. Mix in both sugars until there are no lumps. Set this aside. Put the peeled potato into a large food processor. Using the steel blade, process the potato until finely minced. Drain the yogurt of all excess liquid. Discard the excess liquid. Add the drained yogurt, honey, vanilla, chocolate flavor, and vegetable oil to the minced potato in the food processor and mix on high for 60 seconds. Be sure to scrape the sides of the bowl while processing. Pour this mixture into the bowl of dry ingredients and beat with an electric beater on high for 60 seconds. Be sure to scrape the sides of the bowl while beating. Clean and dry the beaters well. In another bowl, beat the egg whites until soft peaks form. Fold the egg whites into the batter until everything is mixed well. Pour the batter into the prepared Bundt™ pan. Bake in a preheated oven for 55 to 65 minutes or until a cake tester comes out clean. Remove the cake from the oven and let cool for 25 minutes. Do not be concerned if the cake falls slightly. Using a knife, go around inside and out-side edges of cake. Invert the Bundt™ pan over a plate and carefully shake the cake loose. Let the cake cool completely and frost with a chocolate glaze.

Serves 14.

CHOCOLATE GLAZE

1 tablespoon unsweetened cocoa powder
2 teaspoons vegetable oil
1 tablespoon + 1 teaspoon water
3 tablespoons powdered sugar

Combine all the ingredients in a small saucepan. While stirring, bring the chocolate glaze to a boil. Remove immediately from the heat and continue stirring until all the sugar is dissolved. Let cool until thick enough to pour over the cake as a glaze. If the glaze gets too thick to handle, reheat it until you can work with it. The Chocolate Divine Cake does not need any more glaze than this recipe makes.

Nutrition Values

Calories 229
Carbohydrates 41 gm
Cholesterol 0.59 mg
Sodium 168 mg
Protein 5 gm
Total fat 6.4 gm
Polyunsaturated fat 2.0 gm
Monounsaturated fat 2.7 gm
Saturated fat 1.0 gm

Dietary fiber 1.3 gm
Percentage of calories from
   Protein 8%
   Carbohydrate 68%
   Fat 24%

Exchanges
1 bread
1 fat

CRANBERRY CAKE

A friend introduced me to this cake years ago. I loved the combination of the tart cranberries on the bottom and the sweet cake on the top, but I did not love the eggs and butter that were in the original recipe. I am happy to say that this old-time favorite adapted very well to my modifications.

2 cups washed and dried whole cranberries
1 cup granulated sugar
3 large egg whites at room temperature
1/4 cup canola oil, low-in-saturated-fat vegetable oil,
       or light-tasting peanut oil
1 tablespoon honey
2 tablespoons skim milk or nonfat plain yogurt
2 teaspoons Butter Buds® (natural dehydrated butter)
1 cup sifted all-purpose enriched flour
vegetable cooking spray

Spray a 9-inch glass pie plate with vegetable cooking spray. Preheat the oven to 325°. Mix the cranberries and 1/2 cup sugar together in the pie plate. In a bowl, beat the egg whites until very frothy. Add the remaining 1/2 cup sugar, oil, honey, skim milk,

and Butter Buds®. Beat well. Mix in flour. Pour batter over
cranberry mixture. Bake 45 to 50 minutes. Serve warm or cool.
   Serves 8.

Nutrition Values

Calories 229
Carbohydrates 41 gm
Cholesterol 0
Sodium 23.4 mg
Protein 3 gm
Total fat 7 gm
Polyunsaturated fat 2.2 gm
Monounsaturated fat 3.1 gm
Saturated fat 1.2 gm

Dietary fiber 0.3 gm
Percentage of calories from
   Protein 5%
   Carbohydrate 69%
   Fat 26%
Exchanges
   1 bread
   1 1/2 fat

EASY AND ELEGANT CHEESECAKE

No one will ever believe that this delicious cheesecake is
allowed in a low-fat and low-cholesterol diet. This is a great treat
for any occasion and is simple to make.

2 1/2 cups lowfat (1%) cottage cheese
1/2 cup sugar
1 1/2 tablespoons flour
1/2 teaspoon vanilla extract
4 large egg whites at room temperature
1 whole egg (for a lighter cheesecake, eliminate the yolk)
2 tablespoons plain nonfat yogurt
1 pint sliced and sweetened strawberries or
    other kinds of berries
vegetable cooking spray

Let Them Eat Cake

Spray a 9-inch glass pie plate with vegetable cooking spray. Preheat oven to 250°. Using the steel blade, process cottage cheese in a food processor on high for three minutes. Be sure to scrape the sides often. Add remaining ingredients, except berries, one at a time, processing for 15 seconds in between. Pour batter into prepared pie plate. Bake in preheated oven for 1 hour. A temperature higher than 250° will cause ingredients to separate. Turn off oven and leave cheesecake in closed oven for an additional hour. Remove cheesecake and let it cool. Refrigerate when cool. Serve plain or topped with sweetened sliced strawberries. **Serves 8.**

Note: If you want to add a citrus flavor to the cheesecake, decrease the vanilla extract to 1/4 of a teaspoon and add 1 teaspoon grated orange peel, 1 teaspoon grated lemon peel, and 1/4 teaspoon lemon extract.

Nutrition Values (with egg yolk)

Calories 180
Carbohydrates 30 gm
Cholesterol 30 mg
Sodium 328 mg
Protein 12 gm
Total fat 1.5 gm
Polyunsaturated fat 0.2 gm
Monounsaturated fat 0.5 gm
Saturated fat 0.7 gm

Dietary fiber 0.8 gm
Percentage of calories from
  Protein 26%
  Carbohydrate 66%
  Fat 7%

Exchanges
  2 meat
  1 fruit

Nutrition Values (without egg yolk)

Calories 173
Carbohydrates 30 gm
Cholesterol 3 mg
Sodium 327 mg
Protein 12 gm
Total fat 0.9 gm
Polyunsaturated fat 0.1 gm
Monounsaturated fat 0.2 gm

Saturated fat 0.5 gm
Dietary fiber 0.8 gm
Percentage of calories from
  Protein 26%
  Carbohydrate 69%
  Fat 5%
Exchanges
  1 1/2 meat, 1 fruit

FLUFFY FATLESS FROSTING

I do not use frosting very much because it is usually too sweet and fattening for me. This frosting is an exception. It is easy to make, devoid of all fat, delicious and light to taste, and the crowning glory of any cake.

2/3 cup granulated sugar
2/3 cup water
pinch of cream of tartar
2 large egg whites at room temperature
1/2 teaspoon vanilla extract

Mix the sugar, water, and cream of tartar in a small, heavy saucepan. Bring to a boil over a high heat. Continue to boil until soft boil stage— 240°. (A soft boil stage is reached when a very small amount of the thick syrup forms a soft ball upon being dropped into some cold water.) For this recipe the syrup usually has to boil from 5 to 10 minutes.

While the syrup is boiling, beat the egg whites with an electric beater until stiff. Pour the syrup very slowly into the egg whites beating without stopping. Continue to beat until the frosting is thick and the right consistency to spread. Carefully fold in the vanilla. This will frost one layer cake or 12 cupcakes.

Nutrition Values

Calories 43
Carbohydrates 11 gm
Cholesterol 0
Sodium 10 mg
Protein 0.5 gm
Total fat 0
Polyunsaturated fat 0
Monounsaturated fat 0

Saturated fat 0
Dietary fiber 0
Percentage of calories from
  Protein 5%
  Carbohydrate 95%
  Fat 0%
Exchanges Free

FLUFFY FATLESS CHOCOLATE FROSTING

Follow the directions on page 41 and carefully fold in 1/4 cup sifted unsweetened cocoa powder at the end.

Nutrition Values

Calories 46
Carbohydrates 11 gm
Cholesterol 0
Sodium 11 mg
Protein 0.9 gm
Total fat 0
Polyunsaturated fat 0
Monounsaturated fat 0

Saturated fat 0
Dietary fiber 0 gm
Percentage of calories from
   Protein 7%
   Carbohydrate 90%
   Fat 3%

Exchanges Free

FRUIT COBBLER

This lovely cobbler is very low in fat and cholesterol and can be made with many combinations of fruit. If you want a lighter, whiter cake, use 1 1/2 cups all-purpose flour and leave out the oat bran and whole-wheat flour.   If you use canned peaches, drain them and combine the peach juice with water to make 2 cups of liquid.

1/2 cup sifted unbleached all-purpose flour
1/2 cup sifted stone-ground whole-wheat flour
1 tablespoon baking powder
1/2 cup oat bran
1/2 cup brown sugar or granulated sugar

Cakes
• • • • • • • • • • • • • •

1 cup skim milk
1 tablespoon canola oil, low-in-saturated-fat vegetable oil,
    or light-tasting peanut oil
4 cups peeled, pitted, and sliced peaches or apples
    sweetened with about 1/2 cup sugar
2 cups boiling water
1 tablespoon Butter Buds® (natural dehydrated butter)
vegetable cooking spray

Preheat oven to 350°. Spray a 9- x 13-inch pan with vegetable cooking spray. Sift both flours and baking powder together over a large bowl. Stir in the oat bran and brown sugar. Stir in the milk and vegetable oil. Pour batter into prepared pan. Spread the fruit over the batter. Mix the boiling water and Butter Buds® together. Pour the boiling water mixture over the fruit and batter. Bake in a preheated oven for one hour.

Serves 12.

Nutrition Values

Calories 114
Carbohydrates 24 gm
Cholesterol 0.3 mg
Sodium 97 mg
Protein 2.7 gm
Total fat 1.6 gm
Polyunsaturated fat 0.5 gm
Monounsaturated fat 0.7 gm
Saturated fat 0.3 gm

Dietary fiber 1.9 gm
Percentage of calories from
    Protein 9%
    Carbohydrate 79%
    Fat 12%
Exchanges
    1 bread
    1/2 fruit

FRUIT TOPSY-TURVY CAKE

This is a fruit upside-down cake at its very best. The wonderful combination of fresh fruit makes this dessert very moist and delicious. The fact that it is healthy to eat is an added bonus.

10 to 15 pitted and chopped prune plums ,
Or 3 medium-sized, ripe, peeled, cored,
and chopped peaches or apples
1/2 teaspoon ground cinnamon
2 to 4 tablespoons granulated or brown sugar
1 cup sifted unbleached all-purpose flour
2 teaspoons baking powder
2 large egg whites, slightly beaten
1 teaspoon vanilla extract
1/2 cup skim milk
1/3 to 1/2 cup granulated sugar
1 1/2 tablespoons canola oil, low-in-saturated-fat
vegetable oil, or light-tasting peanut oil
1 tablespoon Butter Buds ® (natural dehydrated butter)
1/2 mashed, ripe, medium-sized banana
vegetable cooking spray

Preheat oven to 350°. Spray a 9 - x 9-inch glass or non-stick baking dish with vegetable cooking spray. Mix the chopped prune plums or fruit with 2 to 4 tablespoons of sugar and 1/2 teaspoon cinnamon. Cover the bottom of the prepared baking dish with the fruit mixture. Sift the flour and baking powder together. Set aside. Beat the egg whites, vanilla, skim milk, sugar, vegetable oil, Butter Buds®, and mashed banana together. Slowly combine the flour mixture with the liquid mixture stirring just until there are no lumps. Pour over the fruit mixture and bake in the preheated oven for 30 to 40 minutes or until golden brown. Serve warm or cool.

Serves 9.

Nutrition Values

Calories 183
Carbohydrates 40 gm
Cholesterol 0
Sodium 95 mg
Protein 2.4 gm
Total fat 2.4 gm
Polyunsaturated fat 0.8 gm
Monounsaturated fat 1.0 gm.
Saturated fat 0.4 gm.

Dietary fiber 1.5 gm.
Percentage of calories from
    Protein 5%
    Carbohydrate 84%
    Fat 11%
Exchanges
    1 bread
    1/2 fat
    1 fruit

FRUIT UPSIDE-DOWN CAKE

This is a wonderful way to use your harvest of fresh fruits!

2 teaspoons fresh lemon juice
2 cups peeled, cored, and chopped apples, peaches or pears
1/4 cup lightly packed brown sugar
1/2 cup raisins
1/2 teaspoon ground cinnamon
4 large egg whites at room temperature
3/4 cup granulated sugar
1/3 cup canola, low-in-saturated-fat vegetable oil,
*   or light-tasting peanut oil*
1 tablespoon natural dehydrated butter
3/4 cup + 2 tablespoons sifted unbleached all-purpose flour
vegetable cooking spray

Preheat oven to 325°. Spray 9-inch glass pie plate with vegetable cooking spray. Sprinkle lemon juice on chopped fruit immediately to prevent it from turning brown. Mix in brown sugar, raisins, and cinnamon. Place fruit in pie plate. Beat egg whites until foamy. Gradually beat in sugar. Stir in vegetable oil and dehydrated butter. Gently stir in flour and pour mixture over fruit. Bake in a preheated oven for 50 minutes.

Serves 8.

Nutrition Values

Calories 275
Carbohydrates 47 gm
Cholesterol 0
Sodium 32 mg
Protein 3.2 gm
Total fat 9 gm
Polyunsaturated fat 3 gm
Monounsaturated fat 4 gm

Saturated fat 1.6 gm
Dietary fiber 1.8 gm
Percentage of calories from
    Protein 4%
    Carbohydrate 67%
    Fat 29%
Exchanges 1 bread, 2 fat
    1 fruit, 1/2 meat

FUDGE PUDDING CAKE

Here is a special occasion treat for those of us who love chocolate. The rich chocolate pudding ends up on the bottom of the cake.

1/3 cup unbleached all-purpose flour
1/3 cup stone-ground whole-wheat flour
1/2 teaspoon baking powder
8 tablespoons unsweetened cocoa powder
1/4 cup canola oil, low-in-saturated-fat vegetable oil,
  or light-tasting peanut oil
1/2 cup granulated sugar
4 large egg whites
1 teaspoon vanilla extract
1/2 teaspoon chocolate flavor (optional)
1/2 cup brown sugar
2 cups hot water
vegetable cooking spray

Preheat oven to 350°. Spray a 9- x 9-inch pan with vegetable cooking spray. Sift both flours, baking powder, and 4 tablespoons cocoa powder into a small bowl. In a larger bowl, beat vegetable oil, granulated sugar, and egg whites until blended well. Beat in vanilla and 1/4 teaspoon of chocolate flavor. Stir in flour/cocoa mixture and blend well. Spread batter into prepared pan. Beat brown sugar, remaining 4 tablespoons of cocoa powder, remaining 1/4 teaspoon chocolate flavor, and hot water in a bowl. Beat one minute. Pour this evenly and slowly over batter. Bake 50 minutes. Let cool 20 minutes. Serve warm or cool.
Serves 9.

Let Them Eat Cake

• • • • • • • • • • • • • • • •

Nutrition Values

Calories 187
Carbohydrates 32 gm
Cholesterol 0
Sodium 51 mg
Protein 3.4 gm
Total fat 7 gm
Polyunsaturated fat 2 gm
Monounsaturated fat 2.8 gm

Saturated fat 1 gm
Dietary fiber 0.6 gm
Percentage of calories from
   Protein 7%
   Carbohydrate 64%
   Fat 30%
Exchanges
   1/2 bread
   1 1/2 fat

LEMON POUND CAKE

This pound cake is sure to fool everyone. It has such a rich and buttery taste that no one will guess that they are eating a low-fat and low-cholesterol cake.

1 1/4 to 1 1/2 cups granulated sugar
1/2 cup canola, vegetable or light-tasting peanut oil
1/4 cup honey
1/4 cup fat- and cholesterol-free mayonnaise
*   (Kraft™ makes a good one.)*
2 tablespoons lemon juice
4 tablespoons Butter Buds ® (natural dehydrated butter)
1/2 teaspoon vanilla extract
1/2 teaspoon lemon extract
3 1/4 cups sifted cake flour
1 teaspoon baking soda
1 cup skim buttermilk
2 tablespoons grated lemon peel
5 large egg whites at room temperature

Grease and flour a 12-cup tube pan. Preheat oven to 325°. Beat the sugar, vegetable oil, honey, mayonnaise, lemon juice,

Cakes

• • • • • • • • • • • • • • • •

Butter Buds®, vanilla, and lemon extract together in a large bowl
until mixed well. Set aside. Sift flour and baking soda together.
Beat flour into batter alternating with buttermilk until everything
is well blended. Stir in lemon peel. Wash and dry beaters. Beat
egg whites until fluffy but not dry. Do not overbeat the egg
whites. Stir egg whites into the mixture until well blended. Pour
batter into prepared tube pan. If batter is full of bubbles, tap the
bottom and sides of pan with the handle of a knife to break up
bubbles. Bake in preheated oven for 50 to 60 minutes or until a
cake tester comes out clean. Let the cake cool for 20 minutes
before removing it from the pan. Drizzle the top and sides of
cake with a lemon glaze.
   Serves 14.

Lemon Glaze

> *1/2 cup powdered sugar (Add more powdered sugar
>   to make glaze thicker.)*
> *2 to 4 teaspoons fresh lemon juice (Add more lemon
>   juice to make glaze thinner.)*

Combine the powdered sugar and lemon juice in a small
mixing bowl. Mix until smooth. Drizzle the glaze over the cake.

Nutrition Values

Calories 288
Carbohydrates 50 gm
Cholesterol 0.3 mg
Sodium 88 mg
Protein 4.0 gm
Total fat 8 gm
Polyunsaturated fat 2.6 gm
Monounsaturated fat 3.6 gm

Saturated fat 1.4 gm
Dietary fiber 0.6 gm
Percentage of calories from
   Protein 5%
   Carbohydrate 70%
   Fat 25%
Exchanges
   1 1/2 bread
   2 fat

MISSISSIPPI MUD CAKE

To create this cake, I took one of the original Mississippi Mud Cake recipes and made it healthier. Now you can enjoy this forbidden treat without guilt, but remember it is only for a special occasion.

> *1 cup sifted unbleached enriched all-purpose flour*
> *1 cup sifted stone-ground whole-wheat flour*
> *1 teaspoon baking soda*
> *1/2 cup unsweetened cocoa powder*
> *4 large egg whites at room temperature*
> *1/2 cup vegetable, canola, or light-tasting peanut oil*
> *1/2 cup nonfat plain yogurt*
> *1 teaspoon vanilla extract*
> *1 cup granulated sugar*
> *3/4 cup brown sugar, slightly packed*
> *1 1/2 cups strong coffee, regular or decaffeinated*
> *1/4 to 1/3 cup bourbon*

Preheat oven to 275°. Grease a 12-cup one-piece tube or Bundt™ pan. Powder it with unsweetened cocoa powder. Sift the first four dry ingredients together in a large bowl. Set aside. Beat egg whites until foamy. Beat in the vegetable oil, yogurt, vanilla, both sugars, coffee, and bourbon. Slowly pour this mixture into the flour mixture. Stir until combined. Beat one minute with an electric beater at medium speed. The batter will be very runny. Pour this into the prepared tube pan. Bake for 1 hour and 40 minutes to 1 hour and 50 minutes or until a cake tester comes out clean. Let cool and remove from pan.
Serves 14.

Cakes
•••••••••••••••

Nutrition Values

Calories 250
Carbohydrates 40 gm
Cholesterol 0.14 mg
Sodium 87 mg
Protein 3.8 gm
Total fat 8 gm
Polyunsaturated fat 2.5 gm
Monounsaturated fat 3.5 gm

Saturated fat 1.3 gm
Dietary fiber 1.3 gm
Percentage of calories from
  Protein 6%
  Carbohydrate 61%
  Fat 28%
Exchanges
1 bread, 2 fat

ORANGE CAKE

This moist, dark cake is great with coffee or tea. The subtle orange taste gives this an intriguing flavor, reminiscent of an English tea cake. If you want a whiter, lighter cake, replace the whole-wheat flour with all-purpose flour.

3/4 cup granulated sugar
1/2 cup mild honey
1/2 cup canola, vegetable, or light-tasting peanut oil
1 1/2 cups sifted stone-ground whole-wheat flour
2 cups sifted unbleached all-purpose flour
1 teaspoon baking powder
1 teaspoon baking soda
1/4 teaspoon ground cinnamon
1 cup skim buttermilk
1/2 cup orange juice
Grated rind (zest) of 1 orange
1 cup raisins or chopped dates
6 large egg whites at room temperature

Preheat oven to 325°. Grease and flour a 12-cup Bundt™ or tube pan. Beat the sugar, honey, and vegetable oil together. Set aside. Sift both flours, baking powder, baking soda, and cinna-

51

mon together. Set aside. Mix the buttermilk and orange juice together. Stir the dry ingredients into the honey-oil mixture, alternating with the buttermilk mixture. Stir well for 30 seconds. Mix in the grated orange zest and raisins. Beat the egg whites with clean beaters or a whisk until stiff but not dry. Fold them into the batter. Pour the batter into the prepared tube pan. Bake in a preheated oven for 1 hour and 15 minutes or until a cake tester comes out clean. Cool the cake and remove from the pan. Cover with the orange glaze.

Serves 14.

Orange Glaze

> *1/4 cup powdered sugar*
> *1/2 tablespoon margarine*
> *3 tablespoons orange juice*
> *1 tablespoon orange liqueur, such as Grand Marnier*

Heat the sugar, margarine, and orange juice over a low flame until everything is dissolved. Boil for two minutes. Remove from heat. Let cool slightly and stir in the orange liqueur. Let cool until room temperature and pour over the cake.

Nutrition Values

Calories 308
Carbohydrates 54 gm
Cholesterol 0.3 mg
Sodium 123 mg
Protein 5.6 gm
Total fat 9 gm
Polyunsaturated fat 2.9 gm
Monounsaturated fat 3.8 gm
Saturated fat 1.5 gm

Dietary fiber 2.6 gm
Percentage of calories from
   Protein 7%
   Carbohydrate 68%
   Fat 24%
Exchanges
   1 1/2 bread
   2 fat
   1/2 fruit

PRUNE PLUM CAKE

Here is another fruit upside-down cake to enjoy.

18 to 20 ripe prune plums, cleaned, pitted, and cut
*   into quarters*
3 tablespoons granulated sugar
1 cup sifted stone-ground whole-wheat flour
1 cup sifted unbleached all-purpose flour
1 teaspoon baking powder
1/2 teaspoon baking soda
1/4 cup honey
2 to 3 tablespoons packed brown sugar
4 tablespoons canola oil
2 teaspoons Butter Buds® (natural dehydrated butter)
1 teaspoon vanilla extract
1/2 teaspoon lemon extract
3/4 cup nonfat plain yogurt
3 large egg whites
vegetable cooking spray

Spray a 9- x 13-inch pan with cooking spray. Preheat oven to 350°. Mix prune plums with 3 tablespoons of sugar in a bowl. Set aside. Sift both flours, baking powder, and baking soda together. Set aside. Beat honey, brown sugar, canola oil, dehydrated butter, vanilla, lemon extract, and yogurt together well. Stir dry ingredients into liquid ingredients. Clean and dry beaters. Beat egg whites until very frothy. Mix egg whites into batter. Press sticky dough into greased pan. Press plums, skin side down, into dough. Pour any plum juice left in the bottom of bowl over plums. Bake 30 to 35 minutes.
Serves 12.

• • • • • • • • • • • • • • • •

Nutrition Values

Calories 200
Carbohydrates 38 gm
Cholesterol 0.25 mg
Sodium 89 mg
Protein 3.8 gm
Total fat 4.7 gm
Polyunsaturated fat 1.6 gm
Monounsaturated fat 2 gm

Saturated fat 0.8 gm
Dietary fiber 2.5 gm
Percentage of calories from
  Protein 7%
  Carbohydrate 72%
  Fat 21%
Exchanges
1 bread, 1fat, 1fruit

PUMPKIN CAKE

I have served this cake at our Thanksgiving celebrations for years. You will find that you will use this recipe often because it is delicious and healthy, and it serves a hungry crowd.

1 cup sifted stone-ground whole-wheat flour
1 cup sifted unbleached enriched all-purpose flour
2 teaspoons baking powder
1 teaspoon baking soda
1 1/2 teaspoons ground cinnamon
1/2 teaspoon ground cloves
1/4 teaspoon allspice
1/4 teaspoon ground ginger
1 1/2 to 1 3/4 cups sugar (granulated sugar
*   or a mixture of granulated and brown sugar)*
1 cup quick rolled oats
6 large egg whites
1 (15 to 16 ounce) can pumpkin
1/4 cup canola, low-in-saturated-fat vegetable oil,
*   or light-tasting peanut oil*
1 (8-ounce) can unsweetened crushed pineapple,
*   undrained*
1/2 to 3/4 cup raisins (optional)

Preheat oven to 350°. Sift together both flours, baking powder, baking soda, and spices. Mix in the sugar and rolled oats. Set aside. In a large bowl, beat the egg whites until very foamy. Beat in the pumpkin, vegetable oil, and crushed pineapple. Slowly add the dry ingredients, mixing only until combined. Mix in the raisins. Bake in an ungreased 12-cup tube or Bundt™ pan for 70 to 80 minutes or until a cake tester comes out clean. Let cool and remove from pan. Cover and let sit for a few hours before serving. This cake tastes even better the next day.

Serves 14.

Nutrition Values

Calories 273
Carbohydrates 54 gm
Cholesterol 0
Sodium 133 mg
Protein 5.9 gm
Total fat 5 gm
Polyunsaturated fat 1.6 gm
Monounsaturated fat 2 gm
Saturated fat 0.9 gm

Dietary fiber 3.9 gm
Percentage of calories from
  Protein 8%
  Carbohydrate 76%
  Fat 16%
Exchanges
  1 1/2 bread,
  1 fat
  1/2 fruit

SPICE CAKE

The wonderful combination of spices and natural sweeteners gives this cake its delicious taste.

> 1 cup sifted stone-ground whole-wheat flour
> 1 cup sifted unbleached enriched all-purpose flour
> 1 teaspoon baking soda
> 1 teaspoon baking powder
> 1 teaspoon ground cinnamon
> 1/2 teaspoon ground nutmeg
> 1/2 teaspoon ground cloves
> 1/4 teaspoon salt (optional)
> 1/2 cup canola oil, low-in-saturated-fat vegetable oil, or light-tasting peanut oil
> 2 to 3 tablespoons natural maple syrup
> 1/4 cup molasses
> 1/4 cup honey
> 1/2 cup packed brown sugar
> 1 cup nonfat plain yogurt
> 4 egg whites, beaten stiff but not dry

Preheat oven to 350°. Grease a 12-cup tube pan and dust it with cocoa powder. Sift both flours, baking soda, baking powder, and spices together. Set aside. Beat the vegetable oil, maple syrup, molasses, honey, and brown sugar until smooth. Mix in the dry ingredients, alternating with the yogurt. Fold in the beaten egg whites. Pour batter into the prepared tube pan. Bake in preheated oven for 40 to 50 minutes or until cake tester comes out clean. *Note: Try adding 1 cup raisins to recipe.*
Serves 14.

Brown Sugar Glaze

1/4 cup brown sugar
2 tablespoons water
1 tablespoon margarine or light cream cheese
1/2 teaspoon rum flavor

Combine all the ingredients in a small saucepan. Bring to a
boil over medium heat. Simmer for 5 minutes while stirring
occasionally. Cool and drizzle over cake.

Nutrition Values

Calories 236
Carbohydrates 37 gm
Cholesterol 0.3 mg
Sodium 169 mg
Protein 3.8 gm
Total fat 8.8 gm
Polyunsaturated fat 2.9 gm
Monounsaturated fat 3.9 gm
Saturated fat 1.5 gm

Dietary fiber 1.3 gm
Percentage of calories from
  Protein 6%
  Carbohydrate 61%
  Fat 33%
Exchanges
  1 bread
  2 fat

Let Them Eat Cake
●●●●●●●●●●●●●●●●●

ABOUT COOKIES

Inventing delicious and healthier cookies was the most challenging aspect of writing this cookbook. My house is filled with cookie monsters, though, so I knew I had to create some alternatives that would pass the tests of my own heartless critics. If you have ever baked cookies, you know they are filled with cholesterol and saturated fat. In fact, cookies were probably more responsible for my husband's high cholesterol count than any other food.

I am happy to say that after years of experimenting, I can present you with a great collection of healthier cookies that will satisfy the most discerning tastes of the cookie monsters in your family. There are all kinds of cookies in this book from the wholesome oat-bran variety to chocolate chips. There are even chocolate cookies and brownies for the chocoholics among us. Some of the cookies have a higher percentage of fat than others, but all are lower in fat and cholesterol than the originals. Choose the cookies that fit your dietary needs. By starting your children on these instead of the high-fat variety, you may be extending their lives.

APPLESAUCE COOKIES

This soft, spicy cookie is filled with the good taste and nutrition of apples.

1 cup sifted all-purpose enriched flour
3/4 cup sifted stone-ground whole-wheat flour
3/4 teaspoon baking soda
1/2 cup oat bran
1/4 cup quick rolled oats
1 1/4 teaspoon ground cinnamon
1/4 teaspoon ground cloves
1/2 cup packed brown sugar
1/4 cup canola oil, low-in-saturated-fat vegetable oil,
*   or light-tasting peanut oil*
1/4 cup honey
1 large egg white
15 ounces (1 1/2 cups) unsweetened, all natural applesauce
1/2 cup raisins (optional)
vegetable cooking spray

Preheat oven to 350°. Sift both flours and baking soda together. Stir in the oat bran, rolled oats, cinnamon, and cloves. In a large bowl, mix the brown sugar, oil, honey, egg white, and applesauce together. Stir in the flour mixture. Stir until everything is thoroughly mixed. Mix in the raisins. Spray cookie sheets with vegetable cooking spray. Drop teaspoonfuls of dough about two inches apart onto the cookie sheets. Bake for 10 to 12 minutes. Remove from cookie sheet immediately.
Yield: 50 cookies

Nutrition Values

Calories 49
Carbohydrates 9 gm
Cholesterol 0
Sodium 14.7 mg
Protein 0.8 gm
Total fat 1.2 gm
Polyunsaturated fat 0.4 gm
Monounsaturated fat 0.5 gm
Saturated fat 0.2 gm

Dietary Fiber 0.6 gm

Percentage of calories from
  Protein 6%
  Carbohydrates 73%
  Fat 21%
Exchanges
  1/2 bread

BANANA HONEY COOKIES

This recipe makes a big batch of soft cookies that have a delicious banana taste.

1/4 cup canola oil, low-in-saturated-fat vegetable oil,
        or light-tasting peanut oil
2 tablespoons soft margarine
1 tablespoon Butter Buds® (natural dehydrated butter)
1/2 cup honey
1/2 cup packed brown sugar
2 large egg whites
1 1/4 cups mashed very ripe bananas (about 3 bananas)
1/3 cup skim buttermilk
1 1/2 teaspoons vanilla extract
1 1/2 cups sifted unbleached all-purpose flour
1 1/4 cups sifted stone-ground whole-wheat flour
1 1/2 teaspoons baking soda
1 teaspoon ground cinnamon
1/4 teaspoon salt (optional)
1/4 cup oat bran
vegetable cooking spray

Let Them Eat Cake
•••••••••••••••••

Beat oil, margarine, Butter Buds®, honey, brown sugar, egg whites, mashed bananas, buttermilk, and vanilla together until thoroughly mixed for about one minute. Set aside. Sift both flours, baking soda, and cinnamon together. Stir in the salt and oat bran. Stir the dry ingredients into the batter until everything is well mixed. Chill for one hour.

Preheat oven to 375°. Spray cookie sheets with vegetable cooking spray. Spoon well-rounded teaspoonfuls of the batter two inches apart onto the cookie sheets. Bake for 6 to 7 minutes. Remove cookies from cookie sheets immediately.

Yield: 6 dozen

Nutrition Values

Calories 42
Carbohydrates 7 gm
Cholesterol 0
Sodium 31.6 mg
Protein 0.6 gm
Total Fat 1.2 gm
Polyunsaturated fat 0.4 gm
Monounsaturated fat 0.5 gm
Saturated fat 0.2 gm

Dietary fiber 0.5 gm

Percentage of calories from
    Protein 6%
    Carbohydrates 70%
    Fat 24%
Exchanges
    1/2 bread
    1/2 fat

CHOCOLATE CHIP COOKIES

When you have an urge for a chocolate chip cookie, here is the recipe for you. These cookies are based on one of the original chocolate chip cookie recipes in which each cookie obtained 52 percent of its calories from fat. This percentage was too high, so I have reduced the saturated fat and removed the cholesterol from the cookies without undermining the taste. These cookies are a special treat for that occasion when nothing but a chocolate chip cookie will do.

1/2 cup sifted all-purpose flour
1/2 cup sifted whole-wheat flour
1/4 teaspoon baking soda
3 tablespoons canola oil, low-in-saturated-fat vegetable oil,
      or light-tasting peanut oil
2 tablespoons margarine
2 tablespoons granulated sugar
3 tablespoons packed brown sugar
1/2 tablespoon Butter Buds® (natural dehydrated butter)
2 tablespoons honey
1/2 teaspoon vanilla extract
1 egg white
2 tablespoons mini-morsel chocolate chips
vegetable cooking spray

Preheat oven to 375°. Spray the cookie sheets with vegetable cooking spray. Mix the first three ingredients together. Set aside. In a medium bowl, mix the vegetable oil, margarine, both sugars, Butter Buds®, honey, vanilla, and egg white together until creamy and smooth. Add the flour mixture. Mix well. Stir in the chocolate chips. Drop by well-rounded half teaspoonfuls onto a greased cookie sheet. Bake for 5 to 7 minutes. Remove from cookie sheet immediately and let cool.

Yield: 25 to 30 cookies

Nutrition Values

Calories 59
Carbohydrates 8 gm
Cholesterol 0
Sodium 23.3 mg
Protein 0.7 gm
Total fat 3 gm
Polyunsaturated fat 0.9 gm
Monounsaturated fat 1.2 gm
Saturated fat 0.6 gm

Dietary fiber 0.4 gm

Percentage of calories from
Protein 5%
Carbohydrates 52%
Fat 43%
Exchanges
1/2 fat

CHOCOLATE COOKIES

Kids love to eat these easy-to-make soft cookies.

1 cup all-purpose flour
1/2 teaspoon baking soda
1/4 teaspoon salt (optional)
2 large egg whites at room temperature
2 tablespoons margarine
1/4 cup canola, low-in-saturated-fat vegetable oil,
    or light-tasting peanut oil
2 tablespoons unsweetened cocoa powder
2 tablespoons honey
1 to 2 tablespoons granulated sugar
4 tablespoons lightly packed brown sugar
1/2 teaspoon vanilla extract
vegetable cooking spray

Preheat the oven to 375°. Spray the cookie sheet with vegetable cooking spray. Mix the flour, baking soda, and salt together. Set aside. Beat the egg whites until foamy. Add the margarine, vegetable oil, and cocoa. Beat until the margarine and the other ingredients you just added are mixed thoroughly into the egg whites. Beat in both sugars, honey, and vanilla. Stir in the flour mixture. Drop rounded teaspoonfuls of the cookie dough onto the prepared cookie sheet about 2 inches apart. Bake for 5 to 6 minutes. Remove from cookie sheet as soon as possible.

Yield: 2 dozen

Nutrition Values

Calories 65
Carbohydrates 8 gm
Cholesterol 0
Sodium 57.6 mg
Protein 0.8 gm
Total fat 3.3 gm
Polyunsaturated fat 1.1 gm
Monounsaturated fat 1.4 gm
Saturated fat 0.6 gm

Dietary fiber 0.1 gm

Percentage of calories from
Protein 5%
Carbohydrates 51%
Fat 44%

Exchanges
1 fat

CHOCOLATE MERINGUE COOKIES

These meringue cookies can be made completely fat-free or with some added chocolate. Choose the variety that fits into your diet. Remember to store all meringue cookies in airtight containers or they will become soggy with humidity.

4 large egg whites at room temperature (about 70°)
1/8 teaspoon salt
1 cup granulated sugar
1 teaspoon vanilla extract
1 square (1 ounce) unsweetened chocolate melted
  and cooled slightly
1 tablespoon unsweetened cocoa powder

Preheat oven to 300°. Generously grease two large cookie sheets and dust them with cocoa powder. Beat egg whites and salt until light and fluffy. Continue beating with an electric beater, while slowly adding the sugar until the egg whites be-

• • • • • • • • • • • • • • • • •

come very stiff. (This can take several minutes.) Quickly beat in the vanilla extract, melted chocolate, and cocoa powder. Drop heaping teaspoonfuls of the batter about 2 inches apart on the prepared cookie sheets. Bake one cookie sheet at a time in the preheated oven for 30 minutes. The cookies will flatten out somewhat. Immediately remove the cookies from the cookie sheet, being careful not to break them. Let cool completely and store in an airtight container.

Yield: 50 cookies

Note: These meringues can be made without chocolate. Try using 3/4 cup well-chopped dates instead.

Nutrition Values

Calories 19
Carbohydrates 4 gm
Cholesterol 0
Sodium 9.8 mg
Protein 0.3 gm
Total fat 0.3 gm
Polyunsaturated fat 0 gm
Monounsaturated fat 0 gm
Saturated fat 0.1 gm

Dietary fiber 0.1 gm

Percentage of calories from
Protein 7%
Carbohydrates 79%
Fat 14%
Exchanges
Free

• • • • • • • • • • • • • • • •

DOUBLE CHOCOLATE BROWNIES

I bake these rich-tasting brownies often, but especially to welcome new people into the neighborhood. This is not the healthiest of my brownie recipes, but it will satisfy the pickiest tastes without doing too much damage to the heart. Unlike most brownies, these derive less than half their calories from fat and have almost no cholesterol.

Preheat oven to 350°. Grease a 9- x 9-inch pan.

Sift together:

> 2/3 cup sifted all-purpose flour
> 1/3 cup sifted unsweetened cocoa powder
> Set aside.

Melt together:

> 1 1/2 squares (1 1/2 ounces) unsweetened chocolate
> 1/3 cup vegetable, canola, or light-tasting peanut oil
> (You can do this in the microwave or in a double boiler.) Set aside.

Beat well:

> 6 large egg whites
> 3/4 to 1 1/4 cups granulated sugar, depending on desired sweetness

Beat in:

> 1/2 cup nonfat plain yogurt
> 1 teaspoon vanilla extract
> and the melted chocolate and oil that was set aside

Stir in the dry ingredients until everything is well blended. The brownie mixture will be very runny at this point. Pour the mixture into the prepared pan and bake for 25 minutes.

Yield: 16 very moist brownies

Cookies

Nutrition Values

Calories 141
Carbohydrates 21 gm
Cholesterol 0.1 mg
Sodium 27.4 mg
Protein 2.7 gm
Total fat 6.1 gm
Polyunsaturated fat 1.5 gm
Monounsaturated fat 2.6 gm
Saturated fat 1.6 gm

Dietary fiber 0.5 gm

Percentage of calories from
Protein 7%
Carbohydrates 56%
Fat 37%
Exchanges
1 1/2 fat
1/2 bread

FUDGY MOCHA CAKE BROWNIES

Everyone is always amazed when they learn that these brownies are not laden with cholesterol and butter. They are so rich and sinful tasting that they will fool the most discerning brownie lovers. Remember, these are only for a special treat.

2 teaspoons powdered instant coffee
3 tablespoons boiling water
1 ounce unsweetened baking chocolate square
3/4 cup sifted unbleached all-purpose flour
1/2 teaspoon baking powder
1/3 cup unsweetened cocoa powder
1 tablespoon nonfat plain yogurt
2 tablespoons softened margarine
2 tablespoons canola oil
1 tablespoon Kahlua (coffee liqueur)
1 cup granulated sugar
2 large egg whites
1 teaspoon vanilla extract
vegetable cooking spray

Let Them Eat Cake
• • • • • • • • • • • • • • • • •

Preheat oven to 350°. Spray a 9- x 9- pan with vegetable cooking spray. Mix the coffee and boiling water in the top of a double boiler resting in very hot water. Stir until coffee is dissolved. Mix in the baking chocolate and continue stirring until chocolate is melted. Remove from heat and set aside. (This process can be done in the microwave, but be careful not to let the chocolate boil.) Sift the flour, baking powder, and cocoa powder together. Set aside. Beat the yogurt, softened margarine, canola oil, and Kahlua together. Beat in the sugar and egg whites. Add the melted chocolate mixture and vanilla and beat for 60 seconds. Stir in the flour/cocoa mixture until everything is mixed well together. Pour into the prepared pan and bake for 25 minutes. Let cool and cut into squares.

Yield: 16 brownies

Nutrition Values

Calories 110
Carbohydrates 18 gm
Cholesterol 0.01 mg
Sodium 38.4 mg
Protein 1.5 gm
Total Fat 4.3 gm
Polyunsaturated fat 1.1 gm
Monounsaturated fat 1.6 gm
Saturated fat 1.1 gm

Dietary fiber 0.4 gm

Percentage of calories from
    Protein 5%
    Carbohydrates 61%
    Fat 32%
Exchanges
    1/2 bread
    1 fat

GINGER ALMOND WAFERS

These crisp and spicy little wafers are filled with flavor.

1/3 cup canola oil, low-in-saturated-fat vegetable oil,
*   or light-tasting peanut oil*
1/2 cup packed brown sugar
1/4 cup honey
1 1/2 teaspoons powdered instant coffee
1/2 teaspoon almond extract
2 large egg whites
1 cup sifted stone-ground whole-wheat flour
1 cup sifted all-purpose unbleached flour
1 1/2 teaspoons ground cinnamon
1/2 teaspoon ground ginger
1/4 teaspoon salt (optional)
1/2 teaspoon baking soda
1/4 cup sliced almonds
vegetable cooking spray

Preheat oven to 350°. In a large bowl, mix the vegetable oil, brown sugar, honey, powdered instant coffee, and almond extract until the coffee is dissolved. Be sure that you use powdered instant coffee and not coffee crystals or freeze dried coffee. If you have trouble dissolving the coffee in this mixture, you can warm the mixture slightly on the stove or in the microwave. Make sure that you cool the mixture, however, before adding anything else. Add the egg whites, beat, and set the mixture aside.

Sift together all the other ingredients except the almonds. Gradually stir the dry ingredients into the oil/coffee mixture. Grind the almonds in a food processor and stir into the batter.

Let Them Eat Cake

Spoon half the batter onto a piece of wax paper and shape it into a long roll about 2 inches in diameter. Repeat this process with the remaining batter. The batter is sticky and sometimes needs to be refrigerated before handling. Wrap the rolls tightly and refrigerate for at least 2 hours. (Batter can also be frozen at this point.) When ready to use, cut the dough with a sharp knife into very thin slices, about 1/8 inch thick. Spray a cookie sheet with a vegetable cooking spray. Place the cookies on the cookie sheet and bake 6 to 9 minutes. The thickness of each wafer will determine the baking time.

Yield: 4 to 5 dozen

Nutrition Values

Calories 49
Carbohydrates 7 gm
Cholesterol 0
Sodium 23 mg
Protein 0.8 gm
Total fat 1.9 gm
Polyunsaturated fat 0.6 gm
Monounsaturated fat 1 gm

Saturated fat 0.3 gm
Dietary fiber 0.4 gm
Percentage of calories from
   Protein 6%
   Carbohydrates 59%
   Fat 34%
Exchanges
   1/2 fat

GRANOLA COOKIES

The type of cereal you use will determine the amount of fat in this cookie. Be sure to use an all-natural granola that has as little fat as possible, or experiment with some other types of cereal (Meuslix™ is a good choice).

3/4 cup stone-ground whole-wheat flour
1/2 teaspoon baking powder
1/4 teaspoon baking soda
1/2 cup oat bran
1/2 cup all-natural lowfat granola
1/2 teaspoon ground cinnamon
1/4 cup vegetable, canola, or light-tasting peanut oil
1 tablespoon margarine
1 teaspoon Butter Buds® (natural dehydrated butter)
2 large egg whites
1/2 teaspoon vanilla extract
1/3 cup packed brown sugan
2 tablespoons honey
vegetable cooking spray

Preheat oven to 350°. Sift the flour, baking powder and baking soda together into a mixing bowl. Stir in the oat bran, granola, and cinnamon. In another bowl, beat the vegetable oil, margarine, Butter Buds, egg whites, vanilla, brown sugar, and honey together. Stir this into the bowl of dry ingredients. Drop rounded teaspoonfuls of the batter about 2 inches apart onto a cookie sheet sprayed with vegetable cooking spray. Bake in a preheated oven for 5 to 8 minutes. Remove from cookie sheet immediately.

Yield: 3 dozen

Nutrition Values

Calories 44
Carbohydrates 6 gm
Cholesterol 0
Sodium 20 mg
Protein 0.8 gm
Total fat 2 gm
Polyunsaturated fat 0.7 gm
Monounsaturated fat 0.8 gm
Saturated fat 0.3 gm

Dietary fiber 0.5 gm

Percentage of calories from
  Protein 7%
  Carbohydrates 54%
  Fat 39%
Exchanges
  1/2 Bread
  1/2 Fat

HERMITS

Here is an old favorite that is healthier than the original but just as delicious to eat.

2 large egg whites at room temperature
1/3 cup canola, low-in-saturated fat vegetable oil,
      or light-tasting peanut oil
1/4 cup nonfat yogurt or buttermilk
1/4 cup cold, strong coffee
1/3 cup molasses
1/3 cup packed brown sugar
1 cup stone-ground whole-wheat flour
1/3 cup oat bran
3/4 teaspoon ground cinnamon
1/2 teaspoon ground cloves
1/4 teaspoon freshly ground nutmeg
1/2 teaspoon baking soda
1/2 to 3/4 cup chopped raisins (optional)
vegetable cooking spray

Cookies
• • • • • • • • • • • • • • • •

Preheat oven to 375°. Beat egg whites in a medium-sized bowl until fluffy but not stiff. In a large bowl, combine the vegetable oil, yogurt, coffee, molasses, and brown sugar. Beat until everything is well mixed, then fold in the egg whites. In a separate bowl, mix the dry ingredients together, except the raisins. Combine the liquid and dry ingredients, and stir well. Mix in the chopped raisins. Spray the cookie sheet with vegetable cooking spray. Drop rounded teaspoonfuls of cookie dough onto the cookie sheet about 2 inches apart. Bake for 7 to 8 minutes or until golden brown around the edges. Remove from cookie sheet immediately.

Yield: 3 dozen

Nutrition Values

Calories 57
Carbohydrates 9 gm
Cholesterol 0
Sodium 17 mg
Protein 0.9 gm
Total Fat 2 gm
Polyunsaturated fat 0.7 gm
Monounsaturated fat 0.9 gm
Saturated fat 0.3 gm

Dietary fiber 0.7 gm

Percentage of calories from
Protein 6%
Carbohydrates 62%
Fat 32%
Exchanges
1/2 fat

HONEY DATE DROPS

These cookies are for the honey lovers among us. The dates give each cookie a great chewy taste.

1/2 cup sifted stone-ground whole wheat flour
1/2 cup sifted unbleached all-purpose flour
1/2 teaspoon baking soda
1/2 teaspoon baking powder
1/2 cup oat bran
4 tablespoons canola, low-in-saturated-fat vegetable oil,
  or light-tasting peanut oil
1/2 cup honey
3/4 cup chopped dates
vegetable cooking spray

Preheat oven to 350°. Sift both flours, baking soda, and baking powder into a mixing bowl. Stir in the oat bran. Beat the oil and honey together. Stir this into the flour mixture. Stir in the chopped dates. Drop small teaspoonfuls onto a cookie sheet sprayed with vegetable cooking spray. Bake in a preheated oven for 5 to 6 minutes. Remove from cookie sheet immediately.

Yield: 40 cookies

Nutrition Values

Calories 47
Carbohydrates 9 gm
Cholesterol 0
Sodium 15 mg
Protein 0.6 gm
Total fat 1.5 gm
Polyunsaturated fat 0.5 gm
Monounsaturated fat 0.6 gm
Saturated fat 0.3 gm

Dietary fiber 0.7 gm
Percentage of calories from
  Protein 5%
  Carbohydrates 69%
  Fat 26%
Exchanges
  1/2 fat
  1/2 fruit

MOLASSES COOKIES

These dark, soft cookies are sweetened with brown sugar and molasses. They make a great snack!

1/4 cup canola oil, low-in-saturated-fat vegetable oil,
*   or light-tasting peanut oil*
2 tablespoons shortening
2 egg whites
3/4 cup lightly packed brown sugar
1/3 cup molasses
1 cup sifted unbleached all-purpose flour
1 cup sifted stone-ground whole wheat flour
1 teaspoon baking soda
1 1/2 teaspoons ground cinnamon
vegetable cooking spray

Preheat oven to 350°. Beat the vegetable oil, shortening, egg whites, sugar, and molasses together in a large bowl. In another bowl, sift both flours, baking soda, and cinnamon together. Stir flour mixture into molasses mixture. Drop rounded teaspoonfuls about 2 inches apart onto a cookie sheet sprayed with vegetable cooking spray. Bake in a preheated oven 6 to 8 minutes. Make sure the cookies are not hard. Remove from cookie sheet immediately.

Yield: 5 dozen

Nutrition Values

Calories 41
Carbohydrates 7 gm
Cholesterol 0
Sodium 17 mg
Protein 0.6 gm
Total fat 1.4 gm
Polyunsaturated fat 0.4 gm
Monounsaturated fat 0.6 gm

Saturated fat 0.3 gm
Dietary fiber 0.3 gm
Percentage of calories from
    Protein 5%
    Carbohydrates 65%
    Fat 30%
Exchanges
    1/2 fat

OAT BRAN COOKIES

These cookies will definitely make you wonder how such a healthy cookie can taste so delicious.

1 1/4 cups sifted all-purpose unbleached flour
or whole wheat flour
1/2 teaspoon baking soda
1 cup oat bran
1 cup quick rolled oats
1/2 teaspoon ground cinnamon
1/4 cup canola oil, low-in-saturated-fat vegetable oil,
or light-tasting peanut oil
1/2 cup lightly packed brown sugar
1/4 cup granulated sugar
2 tablespoons honey
1 large egg white, slightly beaten
1 teaspoon vanilla extract
1/2 teaspoon maple flavor (optional)
1/2 cup nonfat milk
vegetable cooking spray

Preheat oven to 350°. Sift flour and baking soda together. Mix in oat bran, rolled oats, and cinnamon. In another bowl, mix vegetable oil, both sugars, and honey together. Stir in slightly beaten egg white, vanilla, maple flavor, and milk. Combine bowl of liquid ingredients with bowl of dry ingredients and mix well. Spray cookie sheets with vegetable cooking spray. Drop small, well rounded teaspoonfuls of dough onto cookie sheets, about 2 inches apart. Bake for 8 to 10 minutes or until golden brown. Remove from cookie sheet immediately and let cool.
Yield: 50 cookies

Nutrition Values

Calories 47
Carbohydrates 8 gm
Cholesterol 0
Sodium 12 mg
Protein 1.2 gm
Total fat 1.4 gm
Polyunsaturated fat 0.5 gm
Monounsaturated fat 0.6 gm

Saturated fat 0.2 gm
Dietary fiber 0.7 gm
Percentage of calories from
  Protein 9%
  Carbohydrates 67%
  Fat 24%
Exchanges
  1/2 bread

OATMEAL RAISIN COOKIES

This oatmeal cookie does not have any cholesterol and has very little saturated fat. It is a dark, chewy cookie that stores well and has a slight taste of molasses.

1/2 cup raisins
1/4 cup water
4 large egg whites at room temperature
1/3 cup canola oil, low-in-saturated-fat vegetable oil,
    or light-tasting peanut oil
1/2 cup packed brown sugar
1/4 cup honey
1/4 cup molasses
1 1/4 cups sifted stone-ground whole-wheat flour
1 teaspoon baking soda
1/2 teaspoon salt
1 teaspoon ground cinnamon
2 cups rolled oats
vegetable cooking spray

Preheat oven to 375°. Combine the raisins with the water in

a small saucepan. Cover and cook over medium heat until all the water is absorbed. Remove from heat and set aside. In a medium bowl, beat egg whites until soft peaks form. Set aside. In a large bowl, beat the vegetable oil, brown sugar, honey and molasses together until there are no lumps and the mixture turns a lighter brown color. In another bowl, mix the dry ingredients together. Pour the dry ingredients into the vegetable oil/sugar mixture. Add the raisins. Mix well. Fold in the egg whites. Spray the cookie sheets with vegetable cooking spray. Drop rounded teaspoonfuls of dough about 2 inches apart onto cookie sheets. Bake 5 to 7 minutes. Remove from cookie sheet immediately.

Yield: 4 dozen

Nutrition Values

Calories 61
Carbohydrates 11 gm
Cholesterol 0
Sodium 45 mg
Protein 1.3 gm
Total fat 1.8 gm
Polyunsaturated fat 0.6 gm
Monounsaturated fat 0.8 gm
Saturated fat 0.3 gm

Dietary fiber 0.6 gm
Percentage of calories from
Protein 8%
Carbohydrates 66%
Fat 25%
Exchanges
1/2 bread
1/2 fat

PEANUT BUTTER COOKIES

Because peanuts contain a large amount of polyunsaturated fat, these cookies will never be low in fat. If you use an unhydrogenated peanut butter, however, the percentage of saturated fat will not be too high.

> *1/3 cup all-natural unhydrogenated peanut butter*
> *1/2 cup honey*
> *1/4 cup canola oil, low-in-saturated fat vegetable oil,*
> *   or light-tasting peanut oil*
> *1/4 cup packed brown sugar*
> *1 large egg white*
> *1/2 teaspoon vanilla extract*
> *1/3 cup quick rolled oats*
> *1/2 cup sifted stone-ground whole-wheat flour*
> *1/2 cup sifted all-purpose unbleached flour*
> *1/2 teaspoon baking powder*
> *3/4 teaspoon baking soda*
> *vegetable cooking spray*
> *1 to 2 tablespoons granulated sugar*

Preheat oven to 375°. Cream peanut butter, honey, vegetable oil, sugar, egg white, and vanilla together in a large bowl. Set aside. Put rolled oats in a food processor. Using steel blade, whirl oats for 60 seconds to make your own oat flour. Set aside. Sift whole wheat flour, all-purpose flour, baking powder, and baking soda together in a bowl. Stir in oat flour. Mix liquid and dry ingredients together well. Chill 3 hours. Form dough into 1-inch balls. Spray cookie sheet with vegetable spray. Place peanut butter balls 2 inches apart on cookie sheet. Flatten to a thickness of

1/2 inch with fork dipped in flour. Sprinkle cookies with granulated sugar. Bake 5 to 7 minutes. Remove from cookie sheet immediately. **Yield: 3 l/2 dozen**

Nutrition Values

Calories 55
Carbohydrates 8 gm
Cholesterol 0
Sodium 30 mg
Protein 1 gm
Total fat 2.4 gm
Polyunsaturated fat 0.8 gm
Monounsaturated fat 0.6 gm
Saturated fat 0.4 gm

Dietary fiber 0.4 gm

Percentage of calories from
  Protein 7%
  Carbohydrates 55%
  Fat 38%
Exchanges
  1/2 fat

PUMPKIN COOKIES

Here is a cake-like cookie popular with both kids and adults. You never have to feel guilty putting these treats in lunch boxes.

1 cup sifted all-purpose enriched flour
1 cup sifted stone-ground whole-wheat flour
1/2 teaspoon baking soda
1/2 teaspoon baking powder
1 teaspoon ground cinnamon
1 cup quick rolled oats
1/2 cup canola oil, low-in-saturated fat vegetable oil,
*   or light-tasting peanut oil*
1/2 cup honey
1/2 cup packed brown sugar
1/3 cup granulated sugar
1 large egg white

Cookies
• • • • • • • • • • • • • • •

1 teaspoon vanilla extract
1 cup pureed solid packed pumpkin, canned or homemade
1/2 cup raisins (optional)
vegetable cooking spray

Preheat oven to 350°. Sift both flours, baking soda, baking powder, and cinnamon together. Stir in the rolled oats. In a large bowl, beat the vegetable oil, honey, brown sugar, granulated sugar, egg white, and vanilla together. Pour the dry ingredients into the honey/sugar mixture alternating with the pumpkin. Mix well after each addition. Stir in the raisins. Spray cookie sheet with vegetable cooking spray. Drop teaspoonfuls of dough onto cookie sheet about 2 inches apart. Bake 10 to 12 minutes. Remove immediately from cookie sheet.

Yield: 50 to 60 cookies

Nutrition Values

Calories 72
Carbohydrates 12 gm
Cholesterol 0
Sodium 14 mg
Protein 1 gm
Total fat 2.3 gm
Polyunsaturated fat 0.8 gm
Monounsaturated fat 1.0 gm
Saturated fat 0.4 gm

Dietary Fiber 0.6 gm
Percentage of calories from
    Protein 5%
    Carbohydrates 66%
    Fat 29%
Exchanges
    1/2 bread
    1/2 fat

RAISIN COOKIES

These soft cookies are a great hit with raisin lovers. For variety, try your favorite dried fruit in place of the raisins.

1 cup raisins
1 cup water
1/2 cup brown sugar
1/2 cup honey
1/4 cup canola oil, low-in-saturated-fat vegetable oil, or
light-tasting peanut oil
1 large egg white
1/2 teaspoon ground cinnamon
1/2 teaspoon vanilla extract
1 1/2 cups sifted all-purpose unbleached flour
1 cup sifted stone-ground whole wheat flour
1/2 teaspoon baking soda
vegetable cooking spray

Preheat oven to 350°. Cook raisins in water until plump—about five minutes. Drain and save water. Beat the brown sugar, honey, vegetable oil, and egg white together in a large bowl. Mix in the cinnamon and vanilla. In another bowl, sift both flours and baking soda. Pour this into the batter and mix well. Add 1/4 cup of the raisin water and stir until everything is blended. Mix in the raisins. Spray the cookie sheets with vegetable cooking spray. Drop rounded teaspoonfuls of the batter onto the cookie sheets. Bake in preheated oven for 8 to 10 minutes. Remove from cookie sheets immediately.
Yield: 4 dozen

Nutrition Values

Calories 60
Carbohydrates 12 gm
Cholesterol 0
Sodium 11 mg
Protein 1 gm
Total fat 1.2 gm
Polyunsaturated fat 0.4 gm
Monounsaturated fat 0.5 gm
Saturated fat 0.2 gm

Dietary fiber 0.6 gm

Percentage of calories from
Protein 5%
Carbohydrates 77%
Fat 18%
Exchanges
1/2 Bread
1/2 Fat

TOASTY OATIES

These are my family's favorite cookies. They taste far richer than they are, and they never fail to delight the cookie monsters in my house.

Sift together:
3/4 cup sifted all-purpose unbleached flour
1 cup sifted stone-ground whole-wheat flour
1 teaspoon baking powder
1 teaspoon baking soda

Prepare:
2 cups quick rolled oats
Measure first, then drop one cup of oats at a time into a food processor. Using the steel blade, process 30 seconds for each cup until oats turn to oat flour. Mix this into the other flour mixture and set aside.

Have ready:
3 large egg whites at room temperature
1 teaspoon vanilla
1/2 cup canola oil, low-in-saturated-fat vegetable oil,
    or light-tasting peanut oil

Let Them Eat Cake
• • • • • • • • • • • • • • • • •

2 tablespoons margarine
1 tablespoon Butter Buds® (natural dehydrated butter)
1 1/2 tablespoons honey
1/2 cup granulated sugar
3/4 cup brown sugar without lumps and slightly packed

Preheat oven to 375°. Beat egg whites until foamy and pale. Beat in vanilla, oil, and margarine until mixed well. Beat in Butter Buds®, honey, and both sugars until all is dissolved. Mix in the dry ingredients. Spoon well-rounded teaspoonfuls onto an ungreased cookie sheet. Bake 8 to 10 minutes or until light brown along the edges.

Yield: 60 to 65 cookies

Nutrition Values

Calories 60
Carbohydrates 9 gm
Cholesterol 0
Sodium 28 mg
Protein 1 gm
Total fat 2.4 gm
Polyunsaturated fat 0.8 gm
Monounsaturated fat 1 gm
Saturated fat 0.4 gm

Dietary Fiber 0.4 gm

Percentage of calories from
Protein 6%
Carbohydrates 59%
Fat 35%
Exchanges
1/2 bread
1/2 fat

FRUIT AND FROZEN DESSERTS

Every low-cholesterol cookbook recommends fruit for dessert. Fruit is a delicious and healthy treat, but sometimes you want something more than just fruit. This section takes ordinary fruit and makes it extraordinary without adding a lot of cholesterol and fat. Each one of the desserts in this section is filled with the goodness of fruit prepared with a little extra flare. You will enjoy these refreshing and unique desserts not only because they are delicious but because you don't have to worry about forbidden fat and cholesterol when you eat them.

THE ALL-AMERICAN PARFAIT

Here's a red, white, and blue dessert for you that is especially popular on the Fourth of July or other American holidays.

> 2 cups fresh blueberries, cleaned and dried
> 1/3 cup brown sugar
> 2 tablespoons honey
> 1 teaspoon lemon juice
> 3/4 teaspoon ground cinnamon
> 1/8 teaspoon ground nutmeg
> 1 pint strawberries, cleaned, hulled, dried, sliced,
>   and sweetened to taste
> 1 pint nonfat vanilla or lemon nonfat yogurt

Combine the blueberries, sugar, honey, lemon juice, cinnamon, and nutmeg in a small saucepan. Bring to a boil over a medium heat. Stir and lower heat. Cover the pan and simmer for 25 minutes while stirring occasionally. Uncover the pan and simmer for 10 more minutes while stirring occasionally. Remove from heat and let cool completely. Chill.

Make sure all the ingredients are cold. Spoon the blueberry mixture into the parfait or dessert glasses. Cover with a layer of yogurt. Top with sliced strawberries. Serve immediately.
Serves 6.

Note: If you want to save time, you don't have to cook the blueberries. Just mix them with sugar, honey, lemon juice, and spices.

Nutrition Values

Calories 170
Carbohydrates 40 gm
Cholesterol 1.7 mg
Sodium 54 mg
Protein 4 gm
Total fat 0.4 gm
Polyunsaturated fat 0.2 gm
Monounsaturated fat 0.1 gm
Saturated fat 0.1 gm

Dietary Fiber 2.4 gm

Percentage of calories from
Protein 10%
Carbohydrates 88%
Fat 2%
Exchanges
1 fruit
1 milk

BAKED APPLES

Here is an old-time favorite that has been made more exciting without adding fat or cholesterol. You and your children will enjoy eating this healthy, easy-to-make, delicious dessert.

4 large apples
3/4 cup Grape Nuts™ or Mueslix™ cereal (or try your
favorite, low-fat, dry cereal)
2 tablespoons honey
1 to 2 teaspoons brown sugar
1/2 teaspoon cinnamon
1/4 cup chopped dates or raisins (optional)
1/4 cup mashed bananas (optional)
1/2 cup apple juice or sweetened water
vegetable cooking spray

Preheat oven to 350°. Core each apple generously but try not to go all the way through the bottom of the apple. Mix the cereal, honey, brown sugar, cinnamon, dates, and mashed bananas together. Fill each apple generously, using up all the filling. Place the apples in a small baking dish that has been sprayed with vegetable cooking spray. Pour the apple juice around the apples. Cover the apples with aluminum foil and bake in a preheated oven for 45 to 55 minutes or until the apples are cooked through. Let the apples cool for 5 minutes, spoon the apple juice from the baking dish over the apples, and serve.

Serves 4.

Nutrition Values

Calories 267
Carbohydrates 66 gm
Cholesterol 0 mg
Sodium 169 mg
Protein 4 gm
Total fat 0.7 gm
Polyunsaturated fat 0.2 gm
Monounsaturated fat 0.1 gm
Saturated fat 0.1 gm

Dietary Fiber 5 gm

Percentage of calories from
   Protein 6%
   Carbohydrates 92%
   Fat 2%
Exchanges
   1 bread
   2 fruit

BANANA BITES

This is an easy and delicious dessert with no added fat.

Juice of 1 small lemon
1/4 teaspoon natural dehydrated butter
4 chopped dates
1/4 teaspoon ground cinnamon
1 to 3 tablespoons brown sugar, depending
   on desired sweetness
2 large ripe, not mushy, sliced bananas
1 tablespoon banana liqueur (optional)
Vegetable cooking spray

Spray skillet with vegetable cooking spray. Heat lemon juice, dehydrated butter, dates, cinnamon, and sugar just to boiling. Add bananas and saute over medium heat for a minute or two, stirring constantly. Remove from heat and stir in banana liqueur. Serve warm or at room temperature. For a different taste, try topping with 1 to 2 tablespoons of cold, plain, nonfat yogurt.

Serves 2 to 3.

Nutrition Values

Calories 170
Carbohydrates 42 gm
Cholesterol 0
Sodium 6 mg
Protein 1 gm
Total fat 0.4 gm
Polyunsaturated fat 0.1 gm
Monounsaturated fat 0 gm
Saturated fat 0.1 gm

Dietary fiber 2 gm

Percentage of calories from
Protein 2%
Carbohydrates 91%
Fat 2%
Exchanges
2 fruit

CANTALOUPE SORBET

This delicious and nearly fat-free dessert can be made with many different fruits. Try honeydew, strawberries, or peaches for a different taste, or be creative and try your own combinations.

1 teaspoon plain gelatin
1/4 cup water
1 ripe cantaloupe, peeled, seeded, and cut into chunks
1/2 cup granulated sugar
2 tablespoons fresh lemon juice
2 cups orange juice
2 tablespoons orange liqueur

Let Them Eat Cake
••••••••••••••••

Sprinkle gelatin over water in a small saucepan and let stand for 5 minutes. Stir over low heat until gelatin is dissolved. Set aside. Puree cantaloupe in food processor. Add sugar, lemon juice, orange juice, and orange liqueur. Blend well. Blend in gelatin. Pour into metal 9- x 13- inch pan. Freeze until mushy. Remove from freezer. Puree the cantaloupe sorbet in the food processor until smooth. Place the sorbet in an airtight container and refreeze until firm.

Serves 12.

Nutrition Values

Calories 69
Carbohydrates 16 gm
Cholesterol 0
Sodium 4 mg
Protein 1 gm
Total fat 0.1 gm
Polyunsaturated fat 0
Monounsaturated fat 0

Saturated fat 0
Dietary fiber 0.3 gm
Percentage of calories from
   Protein 6%
   Carbohydrates 87%
   Fat 1%
Exchanges
   1/2 fruit

CRANBERRY SHERBET COOLER

Here you have a perfect cool and refreshing way to end dinner on a hot summer night. This cholesterol- and fat-free dessert is elegant, yet easy to make.

1 pint of your favorite fruit sherbet—orange, lemon, and/or
*   raspberry are very popular, or try a combination*
1 cup cold cranberry juice
1 cup cold champagne
sliced strawberries or kiwis to use as garnish

Scoop the sherbet into your favorite dessert bowls. Mix the cranberry juice and champagne together. Pour this over the

sherbet. (You do not have to use all the cranberry champagne.)
Garnish with fresh fruit and serve immediately.

Serves 4 to 6

Nutrition Values

Calories 212
Carbohydrates 40 gm
Cholesterol 7 mg
Sodium 47 mg
Protein 1 gm
Total Fat 2.0 gm
Polyunsaturated fat 0
Monounsaturated fat 0.5 gm
Saturated fat 1.2 gm

Dietary Fiber 0
Percentage of calories from
Protein 2%
Carbohydrates 73%
Fat 8%
Exchanges
2 bread
1 fruit
1/2 fat

FRUIT IN YOGURT LIQUEUR

You will not find an easier, more delicious dessert to serve.
We love to eat this in the summer when fresh fruits abound.

1 quart fresh berries, cleaned, hulled, and sliced
Or 5 peaches, peeled and sliced
Or 3 large, ripe bananas, peeled and sliced

If you are using bananas or peaches, sprinkle them with a
little fresh lemon juice to keep them from turning brown.

Sauce:
1 1/2 cups nonfat plain yogurt
1/2 teaspoon lemon extract
3 tablespoons Cointreau, Grand Marnier, Banana,
or Raspberry Liqueur
2 tablespoons brown sugar
2 tablespoons honey

Let Them Eat Cake
• • • • • • • • • • • • • • •

Combine all sauce ingredients, stir well, and chill several hours.
Serve over fresh fruit. Try combining fruits for a different taste.
Serves 4 to 6.

Nutrition Values

Calories 187
Carbohydrates 36 gm
Cholesterol 1.5 mg
Sodium 70 mg
Protein 6 gm
Total fat 0.7 gm
Polyunsaturated fat 0.2 gm
Monounsaturated fat 0.1 gm

Saturated fat 0.1 gm
Dietary fiber 4 gm
Percentage of calories from
Protein 12%
Carbohydrates 75%
Fat 3%
Exchanges
1 fruit, 1/2 milk

PEACHES IN SCHNAPPS

This delicious dessert has very little fat and is wonderful to
serve on a hot, summer day.

1/2 teaspoon powdered sugar
3 tablespoons sliced almonds (optional)
5 large ripe, but not mushy, peaches
1 tablespoon lemon juice
1/4 to 1/2 cup cold peach schnapps

Mix the powdered sugar with a drop or two of water and
stir in the almonds. When the almonds are thoroughly coated,
toast them until they are golden brown. Let them cool. Peel, pit,
and thinly slice 4 of the peaches. Sprinkle the peaches with lemon
juice to prevent them from turning brown. Peel, pit, and slice the
fifth peach. Place it in a blender or food processor with the
schnapps and puree it. Place the sliced peaches in dessert dishes,
pour on the peach sauce, and sprinkle with toasted almonds.
Serve immediately. **Serves 4.**

Nutrition Values

Calories 126
Carbohydrates 17 gm
Cholesterol 0
Sodium 4 mg
Protein 2 gm
Total fat 3 gm
Polyunsaturated fat 0.6 gm
Monounsaturated fat 1.9 gm

Saturated fat 0.3 gm
Dietary fiber 2.3 gm
Percentage of calories from
    Protein 6%
    Carbohydrates 51%
    Fat 19%
Exchanges
    1 fruit, 1/2 fat

PEACH MELBA

This is a lovely dessert to serve at a summer party. You can poach your own fresh peaches or use canned peaches.

1/2 teaspoon confectioners' powdered sugar
4 tablespoons slivered almonds
1 pint rinsed and dried fresh raspberries or
        10 ounces frozen raspberries
2 tablespoons fresh lemon juice
1 1/2 tablespoons confectioners' powdered sugar
3 tablespoons almond liqueur
1 quart all-natural vanilla lowfat frozen yogurt, ice milk,
        or tofu-lite frozen dessert (The fat content of these
        vary dramatically, so choose the one that fits into
        your diet.)
1 can (29 ounces) unsweetened, sliced peaches,
        or 5 poached and sliced peaches
vegetable cooking spray

Preheat oven to 350°. Mix a few drops of water with 1 teaspoon confectioners' powdered sugar. Stir in the almonds until they are thoroughly coated. Spread them out on a cookie sheet sprayed with vegetable cooking spray and bake in a pre-heated oven for about 5 minutes or until toasted. Stir them once or twice. Remove them and let cool.

Raspberry Sauce

Thaw and drain frozen raspberries. Save juice. Place the thawed or fresh raspberries in the food processor. Using the steel blade, puree the raspberries. Rub raspberries through a sieve and throw out the raspberry seeds. Stir lemon juice, 1 1/2 tablespoons confectioners' sugar, and almond liqueur into strained raspberries. If any raspberry juice is left, add 1 to 2 teaspoons to puree. Chill puree.

Spoon ice milk, frozen yogurt, or tofu-lite frozen dessert into individual dessert bowls and top with sliced, drained peaches. Drizzle top of each bowl of peaches with some raspberry puree. (Any leftover raspberry puree may be frozen for another time.) Garnish each dessert with toasted almonds. Serve immediately.

Serves 6 to 8.

Nutrition Values

Calories 198
Carbohydrates 34 gm
Cholesterol 7 mg
Sodium 87 mg
Protein 6 gm
Total fat 5 gm
Polyunsaturated fat 0.5 gm
Monounsaturated fat 1.8 gm
Saturated fat 1.6 gm

Dietary fiber 3 gm
Percentage of calories from
    Protein 11%
    Carbohydrates 65%
    Fat 19%
Exchanges
    1 1/2 bread
    1 fruit
    1 fat

PINEAPPLE AND STRAWBERRIES IN WINE

Here is a dessert with no cholesterol and no added fat that can be served at the most elegant dinner party.

1 pineapple, peeled, cored, and cut into bite-size cubes
1 quart strawberries, cleaned, hulled, dried, and sliced
1/2 bottle chilled white wine or champagne, sweet or dry,
depending on your taste

Mix fruit together. Spoon into dessert bowls. Cover halfway with wine. Mix again and serve immediately or chill for 1 hour.
Serves 8.

Nutrition Values

Calories 101
Carbohydrates 15 gm
Cholesterol 0 mg
Sodium 4 mg
Protein 0.8 gm
Total fat 0.6 gm
Polyunsaturated fat 0.2 gm
Monounsaturated fat 0 gm
Saturated fat 0 gm

Dietary fiber 3 gm

Percentage of calories from
Protein 3%
Carbohydrates 57%
Fat 5%
Exchanges
1 fruit

POACHED PEARS

Try this delicious way to serve pears. The different sauces make this a very versatile dessert.

> 4 pears, ripe but not mushy
> 2 cups water
> juice from 1 lemon
> 1 cup dry white or red wine, depending on what color
>   you want the pears
> grated peel (zest) from 1 lemon
> grated peel (zest) from half an orange
> 1/2 to 3/4 cup granulated sugar
> 1 teaspoon vanilla extract
> 1 cinnamon stick

Peel the pears. Slice them in half and remove pits. Place them in 1 cup of water mixed with 1 teaspoon lemon juice. Set aside. Combine 1 cup of water, 1 cup of wine, the remaining lemon juice, and all other ingredients in a large enamel saucepan. Bring mixture to a boil. Stir. Drain pears. Place them in saucepan and simmer 6 minutes. Remove pan from heat and let pears cool in saucepan for 25 minutes. Remove pears, shake off all excess liquid, and serve at room temperature. If you want to serve the pears cold, refrigerate them for 1 to 2 hours in a little of the wine poaching liquid. Serve pears cold or at room temperature with Raspberry Sauce (p. 96), Marinated Raspberries (p. 101), or Chocolate Glaze (p. 37). The sauce or glaze can be drizzled on the plate to make a decorative design or simply spooned on the plate. Place the pear halves on top. *Note: The French use a combination of port wine, water, and sugar when poaching pears.* **Serves 4.**

Nutrition Values

Calories 174
Carbohydrates 34 gm
Cholesterol 0
Sodium 8 mg
Protein 0.6 gm
Total fat 0.6 gm
Polyunsaturated fat 0.1 gm
Monounsaturated fat 0.1 gm
Saturated fat 0
Dietary fiber 4 gm

Percentage of calories from
Protein 1%
Carbohydrates 75%
Fat 3%
Exchanges
1 1/2 fruit

SHERBET IN CHAMPAGNE

This is such an elegant dessert and so easy to make. I find it is a wonderful way to end a big meal.

> 1 pint fresh strawberries, cleaned, hulled, and dried
> 1 1/2 pints of lemon sherbet or your favorite flavor (Make sure it is low in fat and is not made with egg yolks. I usually buy the sherbet for this dessert in a specialty ice cream shop, but you can make your own.)
> 1/2 bottle of your favorite champagne
> 6 champagne glasses or parfait glasses

Slice the strawberries. (If your strawberries are not sweet, sprinkle a little sugar over them.) Spoon the sherbet into the glasses. Pour in enough champagne so that it fills the glasses half way. Place the strawberries over the sherbet in a decorative design. Serve immediately.
   Serves 6.

Nutrition Values

Calories 192
Carbohydrates 34 gm
Cholesterol 7 mg
Sodium 44 mg
Protein 1.5 gm
Total fat 2.1 gm
Polyunsaturated fat 0.1 gm
Monounsaturated fat 0.5 gm
Saturated fat 1.2 gm

Dietary fiber 1.3 gm

Percentage of calories from
Protein 3%
Carbohydrates 68%
Fat 9%
Exchanges
2 bread
1/2 fat

STRAWBERRY BANANA FROSTED

This is a delightful and healthy way to give the family a frozen treat.

2 cups strawberries, cleaned, hulled, and dried
2 ripe bananas
2 teaspoons fresh lemon juice
1/2 cup nonfat plain yogurt (optional)
sugar or honey to taste

Whip all ingredients thoroughly in a food processor or blender. Freeze until mushy. Spoon into individual serving bowls. **Serves 4.**

Nutrition Values

Calories 97
Carbohydrates 22 gm
Cholesterol 0.5 mg
Sodium 23 mg
Protein 2.7 gm
Total fat 0.6 gm
Polyunsaturated fat 0.2 gm
Monounsaturated fat 0.1 gm

Saturated fat 0.2 gm
Dietary fiber 2.9 gm
Percentage of calories from
Protein 10%
Carbohydrates 85%
Fat 5%
Exchanges
1 1/2 fruit

ZESTY ORANGES AND RASPBERRIES

The marinated oranges and raspberries make a delicious combination, but they can also be eaten separately.

Marinated Oranges

8 navel or temple oranges
2 lemons
1/4 cup granulated sugar
2 tablespoons Grand Marnier or Cointreau (optional)

Grate the peel of 1 orange and 1 lemon and squeeze out their juice. Set aside. Carefully peel and slice 6 oranges into 1/4-inch slices. Squeeze out the juice from the remaining orange and lemon. Combine this juice with the other orange and lemon juice. Place the orange slices in a shallow bowl or platter. Stir the lemon and orange juice, grated lemon and orange peel, sugar and Grand Marnier together. Pour over the sliced oranges. Cover and refrigerate overnight. Turn the orange slices over occasionally. Serve the oranges alone or with the marinated raspberries.

Marinated Raspberries

1 pint cleaned, fresh raspberries
1/2 to 1 cup raspberry liqueur

Place the raspberries in a shallow platter. Pour the liqueur over the raspberries. Let marinate overnight.

Spoon the orange slices and juice into dessert bowls. Drain the raspberries and place them over the orange slices. Freeze the marinated liqueur for another time. Serve immediately.

To make a delicious raspberry sauce, puree the marinated and drained raspberries and strain through a sieve.

Serves 8.

Nutrition Values

Calories 164
Carbohydrates 33 gm
Cholesterol 0
Sodium 1 mg
Protein 1.7 gm
Total fat 0.4 gm
Polyunsaturated fat 0.1 gm
Monounsaturated fat 0

Saturated fat 0 gm
Dietary fiber 4.7 gm
Percentage of calories from
   Protein 4%
   Carbohydrates 76%
   Fat 2%
Exchanges
   1 1/2 fruit

ZABAGLIONE

The rich-tasting cream sauce in this dessert is the perfect compliment to fresh berries. It is important to prepare this mock whipped cream just before serving because it does not stay whipped for long.

*1 quart fresh, cleaned, hulled, sliced, and chilled berries
(strawberries, raspberries, blueberries, and/or
blackberries are particularly nice)
1/3 cup chilled evaporated skim milk
2 tablespoons nonfat dry milk powder
1/8 teaspoon cream of tartar
4 to 6 tablespoons sifted powdered sugar
2 tablespoons nonfat vanilla yogurt
2 tablespoons sweet sherry*

Fruit and Frozen Desserts
•••••••••••••••••••••

1/4 teaspoon grated orange rind
1/2 teaspoon vanilla extract

Place the prepared berries on your favorite dessert dishes and keep them cold. Put the evaporated skim milk in a small bowl and set in the freezer with the beaters from your electric beater for about 15 minutes. Do not freeze the milk. Remove the evaporated skim milk from the freezer and beat in the dry milk and cream of tartar until mixture is foamy. Beat in the powdered sugar, using high speed, until the mixture is thick like whipped cream. Combine the remaining ingredients in another bowl. Gently fold them into the mock whipped cream. Spoon over the berries and serve immediately.

Serves 4 to 6.

Nutrition Values

Calories 125
Carbohydrates 25 gm
Cholesterol 1.6 mg
Sodium 43 mg
Protein 3.7 gm
Total Fat 0.7 gm
Polyunsaturated fat 0.3 gm
Monounsaturated fat 0 gm
Saturated fat 0 gm

Dietary fiber 3.9 gm

Percentage of calories from
Protein 11%
Carbohydrates 78%
Fat 5%
Exchanges
1 fruit
1/2 milk

Let Them Eat Cake
● ● ● ● ● ● ● ● ● ● ● ● ● ● ● ● ●

ABOUT MUFFINS AND TEA BREADS

Now that you are on a journey to a healthier life, you'll be delighted to have these muffin and tea bread recipes. You probably thought breakfast would become boring without those old breakfast favorites: eggs, bacon, sausage, croissants, doughnuts, cream cheese, and butter. What's left? In these muffins and tea breads I've incorporated good, wholesome foods into delicious morning treats. They're filled with a variety of fruits and soluble fibers and bursting with flavor. Breakfast or snack time will never be a bore with these in the house.

I usually double the recipe and freeze any muffins we cannot eat in a few days. In this way, I always have something delightful and healthy to pop into the microwave when I am in my usual morning rush or when I am hungry in the afternoon. Also, this way I spend only half the time cooking.

When I eat these muffins or tea breads with a bowl of fresh fruit, oat bran, or cold cereal, I know I am eating a healthy and delicious breakfast. Since they are filled with good, wholesome food, I find myself less hungry after eating them. And by eating the soluble fiber in them, I am being good to my heart.

Don't save these muffins just for breakfast. They satisfy that 4 p.m. hunger pang too. Both the breads and the muffins make delicious and healthy desserts as well. You'll find yourself eating them all during the day and you can, without feeling guilty.

You should note that when you mix the batter of any tea bread or muffin leavened with baking soda or powder, you combine the wet and dry ingredients just until moistened. Don't beat the batter and you'll have lighter and better tasting muffins and tea breads.

APPLE CARROT MUFFINS

The apples and carrots in these muffins provide you with plenty of fiber and vitamins. These are a delicious treat made even more special by the fact that they contain no cholesterol and just a trace of fat.

Puree in the food processor:
  1 peeled medium carrot
  2 cored and peeled medium apples
Have ready:
  2 large egg whites
  1/2 to 3/4 cup granulated and brown sugar
    mixed together
  1 tablespoon canola oil
  1 tablespoon water, apple juice, or orange juice
Sift together:
  1 cup all-purpose enriched flour
  1/2 cup stone-ground whole-wheat flour
  1 teaspoon baking soda
  1/2 teaspoon ground cinnamon

Preheat oven to 350°. Grease or spray 12 muffin tins. Add the egg whites to the pureed carrot and apples in the food processor. Using the steel blade, blend the mixture for 20 seconds. Add the sugar, canola oil, and water. Blend thoroughly. Mix this into the dry ingredients with a fork just until blended. Do not overmix. Fill the muffin tins about 3/4 of the way full. Bake in preheated oven for 20 to 25 minutes or until cake tester comes out clean.

Yield: 12 muffins

Nutrition Values

Calories 127
Carbohydrates 27 gm
Cholesterol 0
Sodium 83 mg
Protein 2 gm
Total fat 1.4 gm
Polyunsaturated fat 0.5 gm
Monounsaturated fat 0.5 gm
Saturated fat 0.2 gm

Dietary fiber 1.4 gm
Percentage of Calories from
  Protein 6%
  Carbohydrates 84%
  Fat 9%
Exchanges
  1 bread
  1/2 fat
  1/2 fruit

APPLE OATMEAL BREAD

This is a wholesome snack or breakfast treat that will keep you going all morning.

6 large egg whites at room temperature
1/2 cup honey
1/4 cup granulated sugar
1/3 to 1/2 cup packed brown sugar
1/2 cup canola oil, low-in-saturated-fat vegetable oil,
      or light-tasting peanut oil
2 teaspoons vanilla extract
1/3 cup pureed apple (3/4 of a large peeled and cored apple)
2 cups finely chopped, peeled and cored apples
1 cup sifted all-purpose unbleached flour
1 cup sifted stone-ground whole-wheat flour
1 1/2 teaspoons baking soda
1 teaspoon cinnamon
1 cup quick rolled oats

Preheat oven to 350°. Grease or spray two 8 1/2- x 4 1/2-inch loaf pans. Beat the egg whites until frothy. Beat in the honey, both sugars, and vegetable oil. Stir in the vanilla, pureed apple, and chopped apples. Set aside. Sift both flours with the baking soda and cinnamon. Stir in the rolled oats. Stir this into the batter just until the dry ingredients are thoroughly moistened. Pour into the two prepared loaf pans. Bake for 45 to 55 minutes or until a cake tester comes out clean. Let cool and remove from loaf pan.

Serves 16.

Nutrition Values

Calories 222
Carbohydrates 36 gm
Cholesterol 0
Sodium 101 mg
Protein 4 gm
Total fat 7.4 gm
Polyunsaturated fat 2.4 gm
Monounsaturated fat 3.3 gm
Saturated fat 1.2 gm

Dietary fiber 2.0 gm
Percentage of Calories from
   Protein 7%
   Carbohydrates 64%
   Fat 29%
Exchanges
   1 bread
   1 1/2 fFat
   1/2 fruit

APPLESAUCE CINNAMON MUFFINS

These moist, delicious muffins are cholesterol free, low in fat, and great for breakfast and snacks. Why not put one in the children's lunch boxes?

1 cup sifted unbleached all-purpose flour
1 cup sifted stone-ground whole-wheat flour
1 1/2 teaspoons baking powder
1/4 teaspoon baking soda
1 teaspoon ground cinnamon
1/4 teaspoon ground cloves
1/4 teaspoon grated nutmeg
1/4 teaspoon salt (optional)

Muffins and Tea Breads
• •

3 *large egg whites*
4 *tablespoons packed brown sugar*
3 *tablespoons honey*
2 *tablespoons canola, low-in-saturated-fat vegetable oil,*
    or light-tasting peanut oil
1 1/2 *cups unsweetened natural applesauce*
1/2 *cup raisins or chopped dates (optional)*
Topping:
    1 *tablespoon granulated sugar*
    1/4 *teaspoon ground cinnamon*

Preheat oven to 375°. Grease or spray 12 muffin tins. Sift both flours, baking powder, baking soda, cinnamon, cloves, nutmeg, and salt into a large bowl. Set aside. Beat the egg whites until frothy and then beat in the brown sugar until well mixed. Beat in the honey, vegetable oil, and applesauce. Stir this mixture into the dry ingredients until everything is moistened. Do not overstir. Mix in the raisins. Spoon the batter into the prepared muffin tins. Mix the sugar and cinnamon together to make the topping. Sprinkle the topping on the muffins and bake for 20 to 25 minutes or until a cake tester comes out clean. Let cool completely and wait several hours before eating. These muffins taste even better the next day.

Yield: 12 muffins

Nutrition Values

Calories 163
Carbohydrates 33 gm
Cholesterol 0
Sodium 120 mg
Protein 3 gm
Total fat 2.5 gm
Polyunsaturated fat 0.9 gm
Monounsaturated fat 1.1 gm
Saturated fat 0.4 gm

Dietary fiber 2.6 gm
Percentage of calories from
    Protein 8%
    Carbohydrates 79%
    Fat 14%
Exchanges
    1 bread
    1/2 fat
    1/2 fruit

BANANA BREAD

Here is the most popular tea bread made with very little fat.

3 average-size, overripe bananas
1 teaspoon baking soda
1/2 cup granulated sugar
1/4 cup packed brown sugar
2 tablespoons canola oil
2 large egg whites
3/4 cup sifted all-purpose unbleached flour
1/2 cup sifted stone-ground whole-wheat flour .
1/4 cup chopped walnuts (optional)

Preheat oven to 350°. Grease or spray an 8 1/2-x 4 1/2-inch loaf pan. Mash the bananas. Beat in the baking soda. Beat in both sugars, canola oil, and egg whites. Mix the flours together and stir them and the walnuts into the batter just until everything is moistened. Pour the batter into the prepared pan. Bake for 50 to 60 minutes or until a cake tester comes out clean.

Yield: 8 to 10 servings

Nutrition Values

Calories 230
Carbohydrates 43 gm
Cholesterol 0
Sodium 120 mg
Protein 4 gm
Total fat 6 gm
Polyunsaturated fat 2.7 gm
Monounsaturated fat 2.1 gm
Saturated fat 0.8 gm

Dietary fiber 2.1 gm
Percentage of calories from
   Protein 7%
   Carbohydrates 71%
   Fat 22%
Exchanges
   1 bread
   1 1/2 fat
   1 fruit

BLUEBERRY MUFFINS

There is no reason to go back to your old cholesterol-filled blueberry muffin recipe. Everybody will love this new version and no one will miss the extra cholesterol, calories, or fat.

1/4 cup canola oil, low-in-saturated-fat vegetable oil,
or light-tasting peanut oil
1/4 cup honey
1/2 cup granulated sugar
1 teaspoon vanilla extract
1/2 cup mashed blueberries
1/2 cup sifted stone-ground whole-wheat flour
1 cup sifted all-purpose unbleached flour
1 1/2 teaspoons baking powder
1/4 teaspoon baking soda
1/2 cup oat bran
1/4 cup skim milk
1/4 cup skim buttermilk
1 1/2 cups blueberries
2 egg whites at room temperature
Topping:
1/2 to 1 tablespoon granulated sugar
1/8 teaspoon ground nutmeg

Preheat oven to 375°. Grease or spray 12 to 14 muffin cups. Beat oil, honey and sugar together. Stir in the vanilla and mashed blueberries. Set aside. Sift both flours, baking powder, and baking soda together. Stir the oat bran into the flour mixture. Mix half the flour mixture into the bowl of honey and oil alternating with half the milk and buttermilk. Repeat this process. Do not overmix the batter. Fold in the remaining blueberries. Beat the egg whites until soft peaks form. Fold them into the batter. The batter will be very blue at this point. Spoon the batter into the muffin tins, filling each tin about 2/3 full. Sprinkle each muffin with a mixture of nutmeg and sugar. Bake 25 to 30 minutes or until a cake tester comes out clean. Let cool and remove from muffin tins.

Yield: 12 to 14 muffins

Nutrition Values

Calories 176
Carbohydrates 32 gm
Cholesterol 0.2 mg
Sodium 75 mg
Protein 3 gm
Total fat 5 gm
Polyunsaturated fat 1.7 gm
Monounsaturated fat 2.2 gm
Saturated fat 0.9 gm

Dietary fiber 1.9 gm
Percentage of calories from
    Protein 7%
    Carbohydrates 69%
    Fat 24%
Exchanges
    1 bread
    1 fat

BRAN MUFFINS

Everyone has a recipe for bran muffins. This recipe combines my four favorite recipes, and the result is a wonderfully healthy, delicious, and fiber-filled muffin.

3 large egg whites at room temperature
3 tablespoons canola oil, low-in-saturated-fat vegetable oil,
    or light-tasting peanut oil
4 tablespoons honey
1 to 2 tablespoons brown sugar
1 cup 100% Bran Cereal™ or All-Bran™
1/2 cup sifted all-purpose unbleached flour
1/2 cup sifted stone-ground whole-wheat flour

Muffins and Tea Breads
• •

1/2 teaspoon baking soda
1 teaspoon baking powder
1/2 teaspoon ground cinnamon
1/2 cup minus 1 tablespoon oat bran
1 cup skim buttermilk
1/2 cup chopped dates, apricots, or raisins (optional)
Wheat Germ Topping:
    2 tablespoons toasted wheat germ
    1/2 tablespoon brown sugar
    1/4 teaspoon ground nutmeg

Preheat oven to 375°. Grease or spray 12 to 14 muffin cups. Beat egg whites in a large bowl until light and frothy. Beat in the vegetable oil, honey, and brown sugar. Mix in the bran cereal and let stand for 15 to 20 minutes. Meanwhile, sift both flours, baking soda, baking powder, and cinnamon together. Stir in the oat bran. When the wheat bran mixture is ready, stir in the buttermilk and chopped dates. Fold in the dry ingredients and mix until everything is moistened. Do not overmix. Spoon the batter into the prepared muffin tins. Sprinkle the top of each muffin with the wheat germ topping. Bake in a preheated oven for 20 to 25 minutes or until a cake tester comes out clean. If you want to save calories, you can omit the wheat germ topping and still have a delicious muffin to eat. **Yield: 12 to 14 muffins**

Nutrition Values

Calories 159	Dietary fiber 4.1 gm
Carbohydrates 30 gm	Percentage of calories from
Cholesterol 0.3 mg	Protein 11%
Sodium 168 mg	Carbohydrates 69%
Protein 4.8 gm	Fat 21%
Total fat 4 gm	Exchanges
Polyunsaturated fat 1.3 gm	1 bread
Monounsaturated fat 1.7 gm	1 fat
Saturated fat 0.7 gm	1/2 fruit

113

CARROT DATE MUFFINS

Here is a muffin packed with wholesome ingredients and bursting with flavor. If you like carrot cake, you'll love these.

3/4 cup sifted unbleached all-purpose flour
1/2 cup sifted stone-ground whole-wheat flour
1/2 teaspoon ground cinnamon
1/2 teaspoon baking powder
1 teaspoon baking soda
1/4 cup oat bran
2 tablespoons vegetable, canola, or light-tasting peanut oil
2 tablespoons molasses
2 tablespoons honey
2 tablespoons lightly packed brown sugar
3/4 cup orange juice
2 large egg whites at room temperature
1 teaspoon finely grated orange rind
1 cup grated carrots
1/2 cup chopped dates
vegetable cooking spray

Preheat oven to 375°. Spray 12 muffin cups. Sift both flours, cinnamon, baking powder, and baking soda together into a large bowl. Stir in oat bran. Set aside. Beat vegetable oil, molasses, honey, and brown sugar together. Beat in orange juice. Stir this into dry ingredients just until everything is moistened. Wash and dry beaters. Beat egg whites until very frothy and light. Fold egg whites into batter. Stir in orange rind, carrots, and dates. Do not overstir. Spoon into prepared muffin cups and bake for 20 to 25 minutes or until cake tester comes out clean. **Yield: 12 muffins**

Nutrition Values

Calories 129
Carbohydrates 26 gm
Cholesterol 0
Sodium 97 mg
Protein 2.5 gm
Total fat 2.6 gm
Polyunsaturated fat 0.9 gm
Monounsaturated fat 1.1 gm
Saturated fat 0.4 gm

Dietary fiber 2 gm
Percentage of calories from
  Protein 7%
  Carbohydrates 75%
  Fat 17%
Exchanges
  1 bread
  1/2 fat
  1/2 fruit

CORN BREAD

So often corn bread is dry and unappealing. This recipe produces a moist, light, and healthy corn bread that I am sure you'll enjoy.

> 3/4 cup yellow corn meal
> 1/2 cup sifted all-purpose unbleached flour
> 1/2 cup sifted stone-ground whole-wheat flour
> 2 teaspoons baking powder
> 1/2 teaspoon baking soda
> 1/2 teaspoon salt
> 2 to 4 tablespoons granulated sugar
> 2 large egg whites
> 3/4 cup skim milk
> 1/2 cup plain nonfat yogurt
> 2 tablespoons canola oil, low-in-saturated-fat vegetable oil,
>   or light-tasting peanut oil
> vegetable cooking spray

Preheat oven to 425°. Spray an 8-x 8-inch baking dish with vegetable cooking spray. Sift the first five ingredients together.

Stir in the salt and sugar. In another bowl, beat the egg whites until frothy. Beat in the milk, yogurt, and oil. Mix the dry and liquid ingredients together just until blended. Pour the batter into the prepared pan. Bake in the preheated oven for 20 minutes.

Serves 8.

For a different taste, mix into the batter:

1 (8 3/4 oz.) can of drained corn or
3 tablespoons grated cheddar cheese

Nutrition Values

Calories 178
Carbohydrates 28 gm
Cholesterol 0.6 mg
Sodium 322 mg
Protein 5.3 gm
Total fat 3.8 gm
Polyunsaturated fat 1.2 gm
Monounsaturated fat 1.6 gm

Saturated fat 0.7 gm
Dietary fiber 2.8 gm
Percentage of calories from
    Protein 13%
    Carbohydrates 67%
    Fat 21%
Exchanges
    1 1/2 bread, 1 fat

Nutrition Values for Corn Bread with Corn

Calories 203
Carbohydrates 34 gm
Cholesterol 0.6 mg
Sodium 442 mg
Protein 6.1 gm
Total fat 4.1 gm
Polyunsaturated fat 1.4 gm
Monounsaturated fat 1.7 gm

Saturated fat 0.7 gm
Dietary fiber 3.3 gm
Percentage of calories from
    Protein 13%
    Carbohydrates 69%
    Fat 19%
Exchanges
    2 bread, 1 fFat

Nutrition Values for Corn Bread with Cheese

Calories 188
Carbohydrates 28 gm
Cholesterol 3.4 mg
Sodium 339 mg
Protein 6 gm
Total fat 4.7 gm
Polyunsaturated fat 1.3 gm
Monounsaturated fat 1.9 gm

Saturated fat 1.2 gm
Dietary fiber 2.8 gm
Percentage of calories from
    Protein 13%
    Carbohydrates 63%
    Fat 24%
Exchanges
    1 1/2 bread, 1 fFat

CRANBERRY MUFFINS

This wonderful combination of cranberries and oranges gives this muffin a delightful taste. Serves these to the kids as a guilt-free snack.

1/2 cup fresh orange juice
1/4 cup skim buttermilk
1/2 grated orange rind
1/3 cup honey
2 large egg whites at room temperature
2 tablespoons canola oil, low-in-saturated-fat vegetable oil,
     or light-tasting peanut oil
1 cup sifted stone-ground whole-wheat flour
1 cup sifted unbleached enriched all-purpose flour
1 1/2 teaspoons baking powder
1/2 teaspoon baking soda
1/4 teaspoon salt (optional)
1/4 cup granulated sugar
1/4 cup brown sugar
1 cup chopped cranberries

Preheat oven to 375°. Spray 12 to 14 muffin cups. Combine the orange juice, buttermilk, grated rind, honey, egg whites, and vegetable oil. Mix well and set aside. Sift both flours, baking powder, baking soda, and salt together. Mix in both sugars. Slowly combine the dry ingredients with the orange/buttermilk mixture. Mix gently but thoroughly. Do not overmix. Stir in the cranberries. Fill each prepared muffin tin 3/4 full with the batter. Bake in a preheated oven for 20 to 25 minutes or until cake tester comes out clean.

Yield: 12 to 14 muffins

Nutrition Values

Calories 162
Carbohydrates 33 gm
Cholesterol 0.1 mg
Sodium 134 mg
Protein 3 gm
Total fat 2.6 gm
Polyunsaturated fat 0.8 gm
Monounsaturated fat 1.1 gm
Saturated fat 0.4 gm

Dietary fiber 1.6 gm
Percentage of calories from
  Protein 7%
  Carbohydrates 79%
  Fat 14%
Exchanges
  1 bread
  1/2 fat

DARK BANANA DATE BREAD

There are few recipes that are easier to make, healthier to eat, or as delicious as this one is. The banana is used to keep this bread moist, and the molasses gives more flavor to this dark, healthy bread. For a more traditional banana bread taste, try my Banana Bread recipe.

1 cup sifted stone-ground whole-wheat flour
1 cup sifted unbleached enriched all-purpose flour
1/2 teaspoon baking soda
1 teaspoon baking powder
2 tablespoons wheat germ
1/2 teaspoon salt (optional)
1 large ripe banana
2 tablespoons molasses
2 tablespoons honey
2 to 4 tablespoons brown sugar
1 tablespoon canola oil
1/2 cup nonfat plain yogurt
1/2 cup skim milk
1/2 cup chopped dates
2 large egg whites at room temperature

Muffins and Tea Breads
•••••••••••••••••••••

Preheat oven to 350°. Grease or spray one 9- x 5- inch loaf pan. Sift both flours, baking soda, and baking powder together into a large bowl. Stir in the wheat germ and salt. In another bowl, mash the banana. Beat in the molasses, honey, brown sugar, canola oil, yogurt and skim milk. Stir the liquid ingredients into the dry ingredients, until everything is blended. Do not overmix. Stir in the dates. Wash and dry the beaters. Beat the egg whites until soft peaks form. Fold them into the batter well. Pour the batter into the greased loaf pan. Bake in the preheated oven for 50 to 60 minutes or until a cake tester comes out clean.

Serves 10.

Nutrition Values

Calories 190
Carbohydrates 40 gm
Cholesterol 0.4 mg
Sodium 210 mg
Protein 4.9 gm
Total fat 1.9 gm
Polyunsaturated fat 0.7 gm
Monounsaturated fat 0.7 gm
Saturated fat 0.4 gm

Dietary fiber 2.9 gm
Percentage of calories from
Protein 10%
Carbohydrates 81%
Fat 9%
Exchanges
1 bread
1/2 fat
1 fruit

FRUIT MUFFINS

The fruit makes these muffins moist and tasty as well as healthy.

Puree in the food processor:
> *3 peeled and pitted small peaches*
> *1 pealed and cored medium-sized pear*

Have ready:
> *2 large egg whites*
> *3/4 to 1 cup sugar*
> *1 tablespoon light-tasting olive oil, light-tasting peanut oil, or vegetable oil*

Sift:
> *2 cups all-purpose flour*
> *1 1/2 teaspoons baking soda*

Preheat oven to 350°. Grease or spray 12 muffin cups. Add egg whites to pureed fruit in the food processor. Using the steel blade, blend for 20 seconds. Add the sugar and vegetable oil. Blend well. Mix this into the dry ingredients with a fork just until blended. Do not overmix. Pour into the prepared muffin tins and bake for 20 to 25 minutes or until cake tester comes out clean.

Yield: 12 muffins

Nutrition Values

Calories 156
Carbohydrates 35 gm
Cholesterol 0
Sodium 112 mg
Protein 2.3 gm
Total fat 1.4 gm
Polyunsaturated fat 0.5 gm
Monounsaturated fat 0.6 gm
Saturated fat 0.2 gm

Dietary fiber 1.1 gm
Percentage of calories from
    Protein 6%
    Carbohydrates 87%
    Fat 8%
Exchanges
    1 bread
    1 /2 fruit

KAY'S COFFEE CAKE

Try this light cake in the morning with your coffee or tea and then again in the evening after your dinner.

Beat together in a large bowl to make the batter:
    1/2 cup canola oil, low-in-saturated-fat vegetable oil, or light-tasting peanut oil
    2 teaspoons Butter Buds®
    1/4 cup honey
    1/4 cup packed brown sugar
    1 teaspoon vanilla extract

Beat in:
    4 large egg whites one at a time

Sift together:
    1 cup sifted all-purpose unbleached enriched flour
    1/2 cup stone-ground whole-wheat flour
    1 teaspoon baking soda
    1 teaspoon baking powder
    Mix in 1/2 cup oat bran

Have ready:
    1 cup nonfat plain yogurt
    vegetable cooking spray

Stir 1/3 of the dry ingredients into the batter alternating with 1/3 cup nonfat yogurt. Repeat this procedure twice until all the batter, yogurt, and dry ingredients are mixed together.

Mix together to make filling:
    1/4 cup packed brown sugar
    1/4 cup granulated sugar
    3/4 teaspoon cinnamon
    1/4 cup chopped nuts
    1/4 cup raisins

121

Preheat oven to 350°. Spray a 10-inch tube pan with vegetable cooking spray. Sprinkle a small amount of the filling on the bottom. Spread 1/3 of the batter around the pan. Sprinkle half of the filling over batter. Spoon 1/3 of the batter over the filling. Repeat this procedure ending with the batter on top. Bake at 350° for 40 to 45 minutes or until a cake tester comes out clean. Cool and remove from pan.

Serves 12 to 14.

Nutrition Values

Calories 217
Carbohydrates 31 gm
Cholesterol 0.3 mg
Sodium 114 mg
Protein 4.3 gm
Total fat 9.4 gm
Polyunsaturated fat 2.9 gm
Monounsaturated fat 4.5 gm
Saturated fat 1.5 gm

Dietary fiber 1.5 gm
Percentage of calories from
   Protein 8%
   Carbohydrates 55%
   Fat 37%
Exchanges
   1 bread
   1 1/2 fat

MAPLE WALNUT MUFFINS

If you love the taste of maple walnut and thought you had to give it up on a low-fat diet, here's the answer to your prayers. This healthy and delicious muffin is brimming with the flavor of maple walnut, yet it is low in saturated fat.

4 large egg whites beaten until frothy
1/3 cup lightly packed brown sugar
1 cup nonfat milk
1/4 cup pure maple syrup
1/2 teaspoon maple flavor (optional)
3 tablespoons vegetable, canola, or light-tasting peanut oil

Muffins and Tea Breads

* * * * * * * * * * * * * * * * * * * *

3/4 cup sifted all-purpose unbleached flour
3/4 cup sifted stone-ground whole-wheat flour
1 teaspoon baking soda
1 teaspoon baking powder
1/4 cup toasted wheat germ
1/4 cup oat bran
1/4 cup chopped walnuts (optional)

Preheat oven to 375°. Grease or spray 12 to 14 muffin cups. Beat the first six ingredients together. Sift both flours, baking soda, and baking powder together. Stir in the wheat germ, oat bran, and walnuts. Stir the dry ingredients into the bowl of liquid ingredients just until everything is moistened. Spoon the batter into the prepared muffin cups. Bake for 20 to 25 minutes or until a cake tester comes out clean.

Yeild: 12 to 14 muffins.

Nutrition Values

Calories 163
Carbohydrates 25.6 gm
Cholesterol 0.3 mg
Sodium 134 mg
Protein 5 gm
Total fat 5.5 gm
Polyunsaturated fat 2.3 gm
Monounsaturated fat 2.0 gm
Saturated fat 0.8 gm

Dietary fiber 1.8 gm

Percentage of calories from
Protein 12%
Carbohydrates 60%
Fat 29%
Exchanges
1 bread
1 fat

123

MOLASSES MUFFINS

These dark muffins remind me of gingerbread. The molasses gives them their flavor, and the combination of ingredients makes them healthy to eat.

> 1 cup sifted all-purpose enriched flour
> 1/2 cup sifted stone-ground whole-wheat flour
> 1 1/2 teaspoons baking soda
> 1/2 teaspoon ground cinnamon
> 1/4 teaspoon ground ginger
> 1/2 cup oat bran
> 1 cup skim buttermilk
> 1/2 cup molasses
> 1 tablespoon honey
> 3 tablespoons vegetable, canola, or light-tasting peanut oil
> 1 egg white
> 1/2 cup raisins (optional)

Preheat oven to 375°. Grease or spray 12 muffin cups. Sift both flours, baking soda, and spices together in large bowl. Mix in oat bran. Set aside. Mix buttermilk, molasses, honey, and vegetable oil together. Combine liquid and dry ingredients. Stir just until everything is moistened. Beat egg white until frothy. Fold into batter. Stir in raisins. Spoon batter into prepared muffin cups. Let stand at room temperature for 10 minutes. Bake for 20 to 25 minutes or until cake tester comes out clean. **Yield: 12.**

Nutrition Values

Calories 155
Carbohydrates 29 gm
Cholesterol 0.3 mg
Sodium 121 mg
Protein 3.3 gm
Total fat 3.9 gm
Polyunsaturated fat 1.3 gm
Monounsaturated fat 1.7 gm

Saturated fat 0.7 gm
Dietary fiber 1.7 gm
Percentage of calories from
    Protein 8%
    Carbohydrates 71%
    Fat 21%
Exchanges
    1 bread, 1 fat

OAT BRAN MUFFINS

Ever since oat bran was found to help reduce serum cholesterol, hundreds of oat bran muffin recipes have been published. Most
of these recipes are healthy but not necessarily tasty. My oat bran
muffins are not only healthy, but they taste great too! Two of these
muffins and a bowl of oatmeal cereal will give you your daily recommended amount of oat bran.

1 1/4 cup sifted stone-ground whole-wheat flour
1 teaspoon baking powder
1/4 teaspoon baking soda
1 1/4 cup oat bran
1/2 cup skim milk
1/2 cup nonfat yogurt
1/4 cup plus 3 tablespoons of honey
1 to 2 tablespoons packed brown sugar
2 tablespoons vegetable, canola, or light-tasting peanut oil
3 large egg whites at room temperature

Preheat oven to 375°. Grease or spray 12 muffin cups. Sift the
whole wheat flour, baking powder, and baking soda into a large
bowl. Stir in the oat bran. In another bowl, beat the skim milk,
yogurt, honey, brown sugar, and vegetable oil together. Stir this into
the dry ingredients, just until everything is moistened. Wash and dry
the beaters. Beat the egg whites until soft peaks form. Fold the egg
whites into the batter. Pour the batter into the prepared muffin cups.
Bake 20 to 25 minutes or until cake tester comes out clean.
Yield: 12.

Nutrition Values

Calories 146
Carbohydrates 29 gm
Cholesterol 0.3 mg
Sodium 73 mg
Protein 5.2 gm
Total fat 3.2 gm
Polyunsaturated fat 1.1 gm
Monounsaturated fat 1.3 gm
Saturated fat 0.6 gm

Dietary fiber 2.9 gm
Percentage of calories from
    Protein 12%
    Carbohydrates 70%
    Fat 17%
Exchanges
    1 bread
    1/2 fat

OATMEAL DATE BREAKFAST MUFFINS

These hearty and delicious muffins are practically nonfat. They really keep your energy up throughout the morning.

2 cups sifted unbleached all-purpose flour
1 1/2 cups sifted stone-ground whole-wheat flour
2 teaspoons baking powder
2 teaspoons baking soda
1/2 cup oat bran
2 cups rolled oats
1 cup sugar
1/2 cup molasses
1 cup nonfat plain yogurt
1 1/2 cups skim milk
3/4 cup chopped dates or raisins (optional)

Preheat oven to 350°. Grease or spray 24 muffin cups. Sift both flours, baking powder, and baking soda together into a large bowl. Mix in the oat bran and rolled oats. Set aside. Beat the sugar, molasses, yogurt, and skim milk together. Stir into the dry ingredients just until everything is moistened. Stir in the dates. Pour into the prepared muffin tins and let stand for 20 minutes. Bake for 20 to 25 minutes or until cake tester comes out clean.

Yield: 24.

Nutrition Values

Calories 162
Carbohydrates 36 gm
Cholesterol 0.4 mg
Sodium 113 mg
Protein 4.4 gm
Total fat 0.9 gm
Polyunsaturated fat 0.3 gm
Monounsaturated fat 0.2 gm
Saturated fat 0.2 gm

Dietary fiber 2.2 gm

Percentage of calories from
Protein 10%
Carbohydrates 85%
Fat 4%
Exchanges
1 1/2 bread

OATMEAL MUFFINS

This wholesome muffin will start off your day deliciously and nutritiously. It also makes a wonderful snack.

1/4 cup sifted unbleached all-purpose flour
1 teaspoon baking soda
1 cup quick rolled oats
1 cup sifted stone-ground whole-wheat flour
1/4 cup oat bran
3 large egg whites
1/3 cup packed brown sugar
3 tablespoons honey
3/4 cup skim buttermilk
3 tablespoons canola oil
1 teaspoon vanilla extract

Let Them Eat Cake

Topping:

> *Mix together:*
>> *1 tablespoon brown sugar*
>> *1/4 teaspoon ground cinnamon*

Preheat oven to 375°. Grease or spray 12 to 14 muffin cups. Sift the all-purpose flour and baking soda together. Stir in the rolled oats, whole wheat flour, and oat bran. In a larger bowl, beat the egg whites until frothy. Beat in the brown sugar, honey, buttermilk, canola oil, and vanilla. Stir in the dry ingredients until everything is moist. Do not overmix. Pour into prepared muffin cups. Sprinkle a little of the brown sugar topping over each muffin. Let sit at room temperature for 10 minutes. Bake for 15 to 20 minutes or until cake tester comes out clean.

Yield: 12 to 14.

Nutrition Values

Calories 157
Carbohydrates 27 gm
Cholesterol 0.3 mg
Sodium 93 mg
Protein 4.4 gm
Total fat 4.2 gm
Polyunsaturated fat 1.4 gm
Monounsaturated fat 1.8 gm
Saturated fat 0.7 gm

Dietary fiber 1.9 gm

Percentage of calories from
Protein 11%
Carbohydrates 66%
Fat 23%
Exchanges
1 bread
1 fat

PINEAPPLE MUFFINS

This delicious dark muffin is great to eat at any time of the day. The pineapple gives it a tropical flavor, and the wholesome ingredients make it a healthy snack. If you want a whiter, lighter muffin, increase the all-purpose flour to 3 cups and omit the rolled oats and whole-wheat flour.

1/2 cup quick rolled oats
1 1/2 cups sifted unbleached enriched all-purpose flour
1 cup stone-ground whole-wheat flour
3/4 teaspoon baking powder
1 teaspoon baking soda
1/2 teaspoon ground cinnamon
1/2 teaspoon salt (optional)
1/2 cup lowfat (1 percent or less) cottage cheese
2 large egg whites at room temperature
5 tablespoons honey
4 tablespoons packed brown sugar
2 tablespoons canola oil
1 teaspoon vanilla extract
1 cup unsweetened crushed canned pineapple, undrained

Preheat oven to 350°. Grease or spray 12 to 14 muffin cups. Using the steel blade, whirl the rolled oats in a food processor for 60 seconds to make oat flour. Sift both flours, baking powder, and baking soda together into a large bowl. Mix in the ground rolled oats, cinnamon, and salt.

Using the steel blade, whip the cottage cheese in a food processor for 2 minutes—be sure to scrape the sides often. Beat the egg whites until soft peaks form. Set them aside. Beat the honey, brown sugar, canola oil, and whipped cottage cheese together. Beat in the vanilla and egg whites. Stir this mixture into the flour mixture slowly. Do not overmix. Stir in the undrained pineapple. Spoon into prepared muffin tins. Bake for 20 to 25 minutes or until cake tester comes out clean.

Yield: 12 to 14.

Nutrition Values

Calories 178
Carbohydrates 34 gm
Cholesterol 0.4 mg
Sodium 228 mg
Protein 4.9 gm
Total fat 2.9 gm
Polyunsaturated fat 0.9 gm
Monounsaturated fat 1.2 gm
Saturated fat 0.5 gm
Dietary fiber 1.9 gm

Percentage of calories from
Protein 11%
Carbohydrates 75%
Fat 14%

Exchanges
1 1/2 bread
1/2 fat
1/2 meat

PRUNE PLUM MUFFINS

This firm, hearty muffin is filled with goodness.

10 to 12 ripe pitted prune plums
1 cup sifted all-purpose unbleached flour
1 cup sifted stone-ground whole-wheat flour
2 teaspoons baking powder
1 1/2 cups rolled oats
1/4 cup oat bran
1/2 cup packed brown sugar
2 tablespoons honey
1 teaspoon vanilla extract
1 teaspoon grated lemon peel

2 large egg whites
1/4 cup vegetable, canola, or light-tasting peanut oil

Preheat oven to 350°. Grease or spray 18 muffin cups. Using the steel blade, puree half the plums in the food processor. Add the remaining plums and chop them for one or two seconds. In a large bowl, sift both flours and baking powder together. Stir in the rolled oats and oat bran. Set aside. Add the sugar, honey, vanilla, lemon peel, egg whites, and vegetable oil to the plums in the food processor. Whirl the ingredients together until mixed well. Pour this into the dry ingredients and stir just until blended. Spoon the batter into the muffin cups and bake for 30 to 35 minutes or until cake tester comes out clean.

Yield: 18.

Nutrition Values

Calories 147
Carbohydrates 27 gm
Cholesterol 0
Sodium 45 mg
Protein 3 gm
Total fat 3.7 gm
Polyunsaturated fat 1.2 gm
Monounsaturated fat 1.6 gm
Saturated fat 0.6 gm

Dietary fber 1.9 gm

Percentage of calories from
Protein 8%
Carbohydrates 70%
Fat 22%
Exchanges
1 bread
1 fat

PUMPKIN BREAD

This bread is great any time of the day. Eat it for breakfast, dessert, or as a snack.

1 cup quick rolled oats
1 cup sifted all-purpose unbleached flour
1 cup sifted stone-ground whole-wheat flour
2 1/4 teaspoons baking soda
1 tablespoon pumpkin pie spice
1 teaspoon salt (optional)
1/4 cup oat bran
1 cup packed brown sugar
3/4 cup granulated sugar
6 large egg whites at room temperature
1/2 cup canola oil, low-in-saturated-fat vegetable oil,
*   or light-tasting peanut oil*
1/2 cup plain nonfat yogurt
1/3 cup water, apple juice, or orange juice
1 16-ounce can of pumpkin or home-made solid
*   packed pumpkin puree*
1/3 cup molasses

Preheat oven to 350°. Grease and flour two 8 1/2- x 4 1/2-inch loaf pans. Using the steel blade, whirl the rolled oats in the food processor for 60 seconds on high to make oat flour. Sift the all-purpose flour, whole wheat flour, baking soda, pumpkin pie spice, and salt together. Stir in the oat flour from the food processor, the oat bran, and both sugars. Set aside. In a large bowl, beat the egg whites until foamy. Beat in the vegetable oil, yogurt, and

water. Beat in the pumpkin and molasses until everything is mixed well. Slowly stir in the dry ingredients. Blend together but do not overmix. Pour the batter into the 2 prepared loaf pans. Bake for 60 to 70 minutes or until cake tester comes out clean.
Serves 16.

Nutrition Values

Calories 258	Dietary fiber 2.1 gm
Carbohydrates 45 gm	Percentage of calories from
Cholesterol 0.1 mg	Protein 7%
Sodium 282 mg	Carbohydrates 68%
Protein 4.7 gm	Fat 25%
Total fat 7.5 gm	Exchanges
Polyunsaturated fat 2.4 gm	1 1/2 bread
Monounsaturated fat 3.3 gm	1 1/2 fat
Saturated fat 1.3 gm	

SWEET WHOLE-WHEAT BREAD

This dark, moist bread, which is made without eggs, is great at breakfast and is very low in fat.

1/2 cup sifted all-purpose unbleached flour
2 cups sifted stone-ground whole-wheat flour
1 1/2 teaspoons baking soda
1/2 cup wheat germ
1/4 cup honey
1/2 cup molasses
1 1/4 cups skim milk
1/2 cup chopped dates or raisins (optional)

Preheat oven to 325°. Grease or spray a 9- x 5-inch loaf pan. Sift both flours and baking soda together into a large bowl. Toast the wheat germ in a hot oven for a few minutes until it turns golden brown. Be careful not to burn it. Add wheat germ to flour mixture and mix well. Mix honey, molasses, and milk together. Stir this into dry ingredients. Mix until everything is blended well. Stir in the dates or raisins. Pour into the prepared loaf pan and bake for 60 to 70 minutes or until cake tester comes out clean.

Serves 10.

Nutrition Values

Calories 224
Carbohydrates 50 gm
Cholesterol 0.5 mg
Sodium 143 mg
Protein 6.6 gm
Total fat 1.2 gm
Polyunsaturated fat 0.6 gm
Monounsaturated fat 0.2 gm

Saturated fat 0.2 gm
Dietary fiber 4.7 gm
Percentage of calories from
    Protein 11%
    Carbohydrates 84%
    Fat 5%
Exchanges
    1 1/2 bread, 1/2 fruit

ZUCCHINI BREAD

If you have never tried zucchini bread, you are in for a treat. This tea bread is brimming with taste and wonderful ingredients. Everyone loves it (but I never tell my kids it has zucchini in it!)

Combine and mix well:

> 1/2 cup granulated sugar
> 1/2 cup lightly packed brown sugar
> 1/3 cup honey
> 4 egg whites at room temperature
> 1/2 cup canola oil, low-in-saturated-fat vegetable oil,
>   or light-tasting peanut oil
> 2 cups shredded raw zucchini, with skins
>   about 2 medium zucchini)
> 1 (8-ounce) can unsweetened crushed pineapple,
>   undrained

Muffins and Tea Breads
•••••••••••••••••••••••

Sift together:
>1 *cup stone-ground whole-wheat flour*
>2 *cups unbleached all-purpose flour*
>1/2 *teaspoon baking soda*
>1 *teaspoon baking powder*
>1/2 *teaspoon ground cinnamon*
>1/2 *teaspoon ground nutmeg*
>1/2 *teaspoon ground cloves*

Preheat oven to 350°. Grease and flour two loaf pans, 4 1/2 - x 8 1/2 inches. Stir the dry ingredients into the zucchini mixture. Do not overmix. Pour the batter into the prepared loaf pans and bake in preheated oven for 60 minutes or until cake tester comes out clean.

Serves 16.

Nutrition Values

Calories 216
Carbohydrates 36 gm
Cholesterol 0
Sodium 64 mg
Protein 3.3 gm
Total fat 7.1 gm
Polyunsaturated fat 2.3 gm
Monounsaturated fat 3.2 gm
Saturated fat 1.2 gm

Dietary fiber 1.7 gm
Percentage of calories from
   Protein 6%
   Carbohydrates 65%
   Fat 29%
Exchanges
   1 1/2 bread
   1 1/2 fat

Let Them Eat Cake

ABOUT PIE CRUSTS

Making a pie crust without a lot of saturated fat and cholesterol is not an easy task since most pie crusts are made from shortening, lard, or butter. Shortening makes the flakiest pie crusts. These crusts, however, contain high amounts of saturated fat because the fat used in them has been artificially treated by forcing pressurized hydrogen gas through the vegetable oil. The most tender pie crusts are made from lard. Since lard obtains 41 percent of its calories from saturated fat and has 12 milligrams of cholesterol per tablespoon, it is not healthy to use. The tastiest pie crusts are made from butter. Butter, however, obtains 66 percent of its calories from saturated fat and has 33 milligrams of cholesterol per tablespoon. Margarine may not contain cholesterol, but it is usually made from partially hydrogenated oils and, as a result, becomes highly saturated. Given these facts, how can a person on a low-saturated fat and low-cholesterol diet make a good pie crust? It is possible if you combine vegetable oil with a little butter, margarine, shortening, or yogurt. When vegetable oil is used, the resulting pie crust is firmer and less flaky. The reason for this is that liquid activates the gluten in the flour, which toughens the pastry crust. The trick is to keep the gluten down while using as little fat of any kind as possible.

Several methods will inhibit the development of gluten. The first is to use a low-gluten flour. You can create a low-gluten flour by mixing your all-purpose flour with a little cornstarch, oat bran or oat flour. Cake flour has less gluten than all-purpose flour and can be used alone or mixed with other flours.

Since gluten makes a tough crust, you will want to tenderize it when you add any liquid other than fat. A little lemon juice or vinegar added to the dough will tenderize the crust. Yogurt has a similar effect. Egg whites, on the other hand, toughen the crust, as does adding water.*

All liquids used in making a pie crust should be cold because warmth of any kind activates the gluten. Accordingly, chilling the dough before handling it helps keep it tender.

It was very difficult for me to create a variety of healthier pie crusts that were also good to eat. My first experiments resulted in beautiful crusts that were so tough they could have been used as planters for the next hundred years. I began to realize why most cooks gave up on a low-cholesterol and lower-saturated-fat pie crust. After many attempts, however, I have come up with a good collection of pie crusts. Some use more fats than others so you should choose a crust that fits into your dietary needs. Most of the time, I recommend the use of only one crust per pie to reduce the fat and calories consumed.

* Purdy, Susan G.: *As Easy As Pie*, New York: Atheneum, 1984.

APPLE CREAM PIE

This pie tastes far richer than it actually is. It is an easy and much healthier way to make an apple pie.

9- inch uncooked pastry crust
5 cups thinly sliced, peeled, and cored apples
1/2 cup granulated sugar
1/2 teaspoon ground cinnamon
1 cup skim milk
1/2 teaspoon vanilla extract
1 1/2 tablespoons flour
1 1/2 tablespoons cornstarch

Preheat oven to 400°. Place the pie shell in a pie plate. Line the thinly sliced apples around the pie shell. Place them close together but not on top of one another. Beat the sugar, cinnamon, skim milk, and vanilla together until there are no lumps. Take 4 tablespoons of the milk mixture and stir into the combined flour and cornstarch to make a paste. Stir the paste back into the milk mixture. Pour this mixture over the apples. Bake in preheated oven for 45 to 50 minutes. Serve warm or cold.
Serves 8.

Nutrition Values

Calories 217
Carbohydrates 39 gm
Cholesterol 0.5 mg
Sodium 180 mg
Protein 2.7 gm
Total fat 6.3 gm
Polyunsaturated fat 1.6 gm
Monounsaturated fat 2.5 gm
Saturated fat 1.5 gm

Dietary fiber 3.1 gm
Percent of calories from:
Protein 5%
Carbohydrates 70%
Fat 25%
Exchanges
1 bread
1 fat
1 fruit

APPLE CRISP

This is an easy, healthy, and delicious way to serve a dessert. For a more traditional crisp topping, replace the rolled oats and oat bran with 2/3 cup all-purpose flour.

6 large peeled and cored apples
2 tablespoons honey
2 tablespoons brown sugar
1 teaspoon ground cinnamon
1/3 cup quick rolled oats
1/3 cup oat bran
1 teaspoon ground cinnamon
2 tablespoons canola oil
1/2 cup packed brown sugar
1 tablespoon honey
vegetable cooking spray

Preheat oven to 350°. Spray a 2-quart baking dish with vegetable cooking spray. Slice apples. Put them in baking dish and then mix in 2 tablespoons honey, 2 tablespoons brown sugar, and 1 teaspoon cinnamon. Set aside. Mix rolled oats, oat bran, cinnamon, canola oil, brown sugar, and honey. Sprinkle over apples. Bake 30 to 35 minutes. **Serves 6 to 8.**

Nutrition Values

Calories 263	Saturated fat 0.9 gm
Carbohydrates 57 gm	Dietary fiber 3.3 gm
Cholesterol 0	Percent of calories from:
Sodium 8 mg	Protein 3%
Protein 1.8 gm	Carbohydrates 80%
Total fat 5.6 gm	Fat 18%
Polyunsaturated fat 1.8 gm	Exchanges, 1/2 bread, 1 fat,
Monounsaturated fat 2.3 gm	1 1/2 fruit

APRICOT CREAM PIE

Now you can have a cream pie that will fit into your diet.
The texture is smooth and creamy, and it tastes far richer than it
actually is.

> 2 cups nonfat plain yogurt
> 9-inch pastry crust, unbaked
> 1 cup dried apricot halves
> 3 tablespoons lowfat (1% or less) cottage cheese
> 3 large egg whites at room temperature
> 3 tablespoons honey
> 1/3 to 1/2 cup granulated sugar
> 1/4 cup all-purpose unbleached flour
> grated rind (zest) of 1 orange
> 1/2 teaspoon vanilla extract
> 1/4 teaspoon lemon extract

Pour 2 cups of yogurt into a colander lined with cheesecloth. Let yogurt drain while raised over a bowl for at least 4
hours in the refrigerator. Discard liquid in bowl. Preheat oven to
375°. Roll out pie dough. Line a pie plate with dough, and chill
until ready to use. Chop apricots. Place them in a saucepan and
cover with water. Simmer 10 minutes and drain.

Using a steel blade, whirl cottage cheese and drained
yogurt in food processor for one minute or until completely
smooth. Whirl in each egg white, one at a time. Add rest of
ingredients, except apricots and pie crust, and process for 30
seconds. Add apricots and process with an on/off touch five
times or until the apricots are chopped. Pour the apricot mixture
into the pie crust and bake for 40 to 45 minutes. Cool. Serve cold
or at room temperature. Refrigerate leftover pie. **Serves 8.**

Let Them Eat Cake

Nutrition Values

Calories 293
Carbohydrates 53 gm
Cholesterol 1.2 mg
Sodium 251 mg
Protein 8.2 gm
Total fat 6.1 gm
Polyunsaturated fat 1.5 gm
Monounsaturated fat 2.5 gm
Saturated fat 1.5 gm

Dietary fiber 2.1 gm
Percent of calories from:
  Protein 11%
  Carbohydrates 71%
  Fat 19%
Exchanges, 1 1/2 bread, 1 fat
  1 fruit, 1/2 meat
  1/2 milk

BLUEBERRY CUSTARD PIE

Blueberries always remind me of hot summer days and cool berry pies. Here is a new and healthy way to enjoy those berries, any time of the year.

2 1/2 cups fresh blueberries
1 tablespoon granulated sugar
1/3 cup skim milk
1/3 cup lowfat (1%) cottage cheese
1/4 to 1/3 cup granulated sugar
1/4 cup unbleached all-purpose flour
1/2 teaspoon ground cinnamon
1/4 teaspoon grated lemon rind (zest)
2 large egg whites
vegetable cooking spray

Preheat oven to 375°. Spread the blueberries in a 9-inch glass pie plate sprayed with vegetable cooking spray. Sprinkle with 1 tablespoon sugar. In a food processor, beat the milk and

142

cottage cheese together until very creamy. Add the other ingredients, one at a time, processing for 10 seconds after each addition. Top the blueberries with the custard mixture. Place the pie plate in a pan of hot water, making sure the water does not get into the pie. Bake for 40 minutes. Cool and serve or serve cold. Refrigerate after serving.

Serves 6.

Nutrition Values

Calories 118
Carbohydrates 26 gm
Cholesterol 0.8 mg
Sodium 80 mg
Protein 4 gm
Total Fat 0.4 gm
Polyunsaturated fat 0.1 gm
Monounsaturated fat 0.1 gm
Saturated fat 0.1 gm

Dietary fiber 1.5 gm
Percent of calories from:
  Protein 13%
  Carbohydrates 84%
  Fat 3%
Exchanges
  1 fruit
  1/2 meat

DEEP-DISH PEACH PIE

This pie lets the natural goodness of the peaches shine through.

> 3 lbs. ripe, not mushy, peaches, peeled, pitted,
>   and thinly sliced
> 3/4 cup brown, granulated, or mixed sugar
> 3 tablespoons quick cooking tapioca
> 1/2 teaspoon ground cinnamon
> 1/2 teaspoon almond extract
> 1 teaspoon lemon juice
> 9-inch unbaked pie crust
> vegetable cooking spray

Preheat oven to 375°. Mix the first six ingredients together. Let stand for 15 minutes, stirring occasionally. Spray 9-inch glass pie dish with vegetable cooking spray. Pour in the peach mixture. Roll out the pie crust dough. Cover the peaches with the pie crust dough. Pierce the pie crust dough with a fork. Bake for 40 minutes or until golden brown.

Serves 8.

Nutrition Values

Calories 256
Carbohydrates 51 gm
Cholesterol 0
Sodium 169 mg
Protein 2.4 gm
Total fat 6 gm
Polyunsaturated fat 1.5 gm
Monounsaturated fat 2.5 gm
Saturated fat 1.4 gm

Dietary fiber 3.3 gm
Percent of calories from:
   Protein 4%
   Carbohydrates 76%
   Fat 20%
Exchanges:
   1 bread
   1 fat
   1 1/2 fruit

FRUIT TART

Eating fresh fruit is a healthy and natural way to add fiber to your diet and lower your cholesterol. Here is a colorful and delicious tart that adds an exotic combination of fresh fruits to your diet.

4 ripe kiwi, peeled and sliced into quarter-inch slices
1 pint strawberries, cleaned, hulled, dried, and sliced
2 tablespoons granulated sugar
1 medium to large lemon
1 teaspoon grated orange rind (zest)
3/4 cup fresh orange juice
1 1/2 tablespoons quick tapioca
2 tablespoons apricot jam
1 tablespoon Grand Marnier, Cointreau, Raspberry
        Liqueur, Banana Liqueur, or orange juice
2 ripe but firm bananas
1 teaspoon granulated sugar
10-inch pastry crust, baked and cooled

Place the sliced kiwi and strawberries in separate flat bowls or baking dishes. Sprinkle each with 1 tablespoon granulated sugar. Squeeze out the juice of half of the lemon and sprinkle evenly over each bowl. Stir. Let sit for 30 minutes, stirring occasionally. Combine the grated orange rind, orange juice, tapioca, and apricot jam in a small, heavy saucepan. Bring to a boil. Stir and simmer for ten minutes. Stir in the liqueur or the tablespoon of orange juice. Let cool slightly. Strain the kiwi and strawberries and mix the strained juice into the glaze in the saucepan. Slice the bananas. Toss the sliced bananas with 1 teaspoon fresh lemon juice and 1 teaspoon granulated sugar.

Let Them Eat Cake
● ● ● ● ● ● ● ● ● ● ● ● ● ● ● ● ●

Brush the bottom of the prebaked and cooled pie crust with some of the apricot glaze. Arrange the sliced bananas in the bottom of the pie. Brush them with part of the glaze. Arrange the kiwi over the bananas. Brush them with some glaze. Arrange the strawberries on the top. Spoon on the rest of the glaze. Refrigerate for one hour and serve immediately.
Serves 8.

Note: Because this pie uses fresh bananas, it needs to be eaten the same day it is made. If you are on a very low fat diet or counting calories, just omit the pie crust and serve the fruit and glaze in individual parfait dishes.

Nutrition Values

Calories 205
Carbohydrates 36 gm
Cholesterol 0 mg
Sodium 166 mg
Protein 2.4 gm
Total Fat 6 gm
Polyunsaturated fat 1.5 gm
Monounsaturated fat 2.5 gm
Saturated fat 1.5 gm

Dietary fiber 3.5 gm
Percent of calories from:
    Protein 4%
    Carbohydrates 67%
    Fat 27%
Exchanges
    1 bread
    1 fat
    1 1/2 fruit

LOWER FAT PIE CRUST

I have reduced the amount of fat and cholesterol to the lowest denominator in this pie crust. Even so, it is a delicious pie crust that no one will know has been modified. As with all pie crusts, handle the dough as little as possible and keep it cold. Heat activates the gluten and makes the crust tough. Do not add water to this crust.

> 3/4 cup minus 1 tablespoon sifted, all-purpose
> unbleached flour
> 1/2 cup minus 1 tablespoon stone-ground whole-
> wheat flour (If you want a lighter crust, replace
> the whole-wheat flour with all-purpose flour)
> 1 1/2 tablespoons cornstarch
> 2 tablespoons canola oil
> 1 tablespoon shortening, margarine, or butter
> 1 teaspoon honey
> 1 to 2 teaspoons lemon juice
> 1 teaspoon grated orange rind
> 2 to 2 1/2 tablespoons plain nonfat cold yogurt

Sift the dry ingredients together. Mix in the canola oil, shortening, honey, lemon juice, and grated orange rind. Add just enough nonfat yogurt to form the dough into a ball that can be rolled out. Chill the dough 10 minutes. Roll the dough out on a lightly floured piece of waxed paper. Keep the rolling pin lightly floured. If the dough is hard to handle, let it stand at room temperature for a few minutes. When the circumference of the dough is one inch bigger than the pie plate, invert the dough into a 9- or 10-inch pie plate. Carefully remove the wax paper. Refrigerate the dough until ready to use.

Nutrition Values

Calories 110
Carbohydrates 15 gm
Cholesterol 0.08 mg
Sodium 23 mg
Protein 1.9 gm
Total fat 5 gm
Polyunsaturated fat 1.8 gm
Monounsaturated fat 2.1 gm
Saturated fat 0.8 gm

Dietary fiber 1.1 gm
Percent of calories from
    Protein 7%
    Carbohydrates 53%
    Fat 40%
Exchanges
    1 bread
    1 fat

ORANGE KIWI PIE

I love to serve this pie. It is beautiful and nutritious. You'll get a flood of compliments when you bring this to the table, and everyone will want the recipe.

10-inch unbaked pastry crust, cold
1 large egg white, slightly beaten
5 navel oranges, peeled and separated into segments
5 ripe kiwi, peeled and sliced into quarter-inch slices
juice of 1/2 lemon
1 tablespoon granulated sugar
1/2 cup fresh orange juice
1/2 teaspoon grated orange peel (zest)
1 tablespoon minute tapioca
1 tablespoon + 2 teaspoons apricot jelly or jam
1 tablespoon Grand Marnier, Cointreau, or orange juice
vegetable cooking spray

Pies

• • • • • • • • • • • • • •

Baking an Empty Pie Crust

Preheat oven to 400°. Roll out the cold dough on a well-floured piece of waxed paper using a well-floured rolling pin. Keep the rolling pin floured. When the circumference of the dough is an inch bigger than the pie plate, invert the dough into the pie plate. Form the dough to fit the pie plate and prick the dough all over with a fork. Spray the shiny side of a piece of aluminum foil with vegetable cooking spray and place it over the dough—shiny side down. Weigh the foil down with pie weights, rice, beans, or a smaller pie plate. Bake at 400° for 8 minutes. Remove the pie plate and lower the oven temperature to 350°. Brush the pie crust with the beaten egg white. Return it to the oven and bake 5 to 10 minutes more or until golden. If the crust starts browning too much, just cover all of it with the aluminum foil. Let cool completely.

Place the orange sections and sliced kiwi in a flat bowl or glass baking dish. Sprinkle with the lemon juice and 1 tablespoon of sugar. Let sit for 30 minutes, carefully stirring occasionally. Combine the orange juice, orange peel, tapioca, and apricot jam in a small, heavy saucepan. Bring to a boil over a medium flame. While stirring regularly, simmer for 10 minutes. Remove from heat. Stir in the liqueur or tablespoon of orange juice. Let cool. Strain the oranges and kiwi. Stir the strained liquid into the apricot sauce. Brush a little of the apricot sauce on the baked 10-inch pie crust. Next, place the kiwi on the bottom and sides of the pie crust. Arrange the orange sections decoratively over the kiwi. Spoon the apricot sauce over the oranges. Cover and chill for 2 hours. Serve cold.
Serves 8.

Nutrition Values

Calories 193
Carbohydrates 32 gm
Cholesterol 0
Sodium 173 mg
Protein 3 gm
Total fat 6 gm
Polyunsaturated fat 1.5 gm
Monounsaturated fat 2.5 gm
Saturated fat 1.4 gm

Dietary fiber 4.2 gm
Percent of calories from
   Protein 6%
   Carbohydrates 65%
   Fat 28%
Exchanges
   1 bread
   1 fat
   1 Fruit

PASTRY CRUST

This is my favorite pie crust because of its light taste and the way it handles so easily. I use it for my cream pies or any other pie that requires a light, delicate crust. Remember not to add water to this crust and handle it as little as possible.

1 cup minus 1 level tablespoon sifted, all-purpose
        unbleached flour
3 tablespoons cake flour
1 tablespoon cornstarch
2 teaspoons honey
3 tablespoons canola oil
1 tablespoon shortening
1 tablespoon plain nonfat cold yogurt
1 teaspoon lemon juice
1 teaspoon grated orange peel

Sift both flours and cornstarch together. Mix in the other ingredients. Form into a ball. Chill 10 minutes. Roll out the dough on a well-floured piece of waxed paper with a floured rolling pin. Keep the rolling pin floured. When the circumfer-

ence of the dough is 1 inch bigger than the pie plate, invert the
dough into a 9- or 10-inch pie plate. Remove the waxed paper
carefully.

Nutrition Values

Calories 125
Carbohydrates 14 gm
Cholesterol 0.03 mg
Sodium 2 mg
Protein 1.4 gm
Total fat 6.8 gm
Polyunsaturated fat 2.1 gm
Monounsaturated fat 3.1 gm

Saturated fat 1.3 gm
Dietary fiber 0.4 gm
Percent of calories from
   Protein 4%
   Carbohydrates 47%
   Fat 49%
Exchanges
   1 bread, 1 1/2 fat

PEACH CRUMB PIE

You'll enjoy this new, healthy peach pie.

8 medium peaches, peeled, cored and slices
juice of 1 lemon
1/4 cup lightly packed brown sugar
2 tablespoons honey
1/8 teaspoon ground cinnamon
1/8 teaspoon ground nutmeg
3 tablespoons quick cooking tapioca or flour
Yogurt Crumb Pie Topping (see page 162)
vegetable cooking spray

Preheat oven to 350°. Spray 9-inch glass pie plate with
vegetable cooking spray. Sprinkle lemon over the peaches as you
slice them. Toss the peaches, lemon juice, brown sugar, honey,
spices, and tapioca together. Let stand for 15 minutes. Pour into
the pie plate and cover with Yogurt Crumb Pie Topping. Bake in
a preheated over for 45 to 50 minutes. **Serves 8**

Nutrition Values

Calories 174
Carbohydrates 36 gm
Cholesterol 0.3 mg
Sodium 32 mg
Protein 2.1 gm
Total fat 3.4 gm
Polyunsaturated fat 1.1 gm
Monounsaturated fat 1.5 gm
Saturated fat 0.6 gm

Dietary fiber 1.8 gm
Percent of calories from
   Protein 5%
   Carbohydrates 79%
   Fat 17%
Exchanges
   1 fat
   1 Fruit

PEAR PIE

I love pears, and I really enjoy this recipe because it gives me a new, healthy, and delicious way to eat them.

1 9-inch unbaked pastry crust or Apple Crisp Topping
6 ripe but firm pears, peeled, cored, and sliced
juice from 1/2 lemon
2 tablespoons granulated sugar
2 tablespoons brown sugar
1 tablespoon honey
1 tablespoon cornstarch
1 tablespoon flour
1/4 teaspoon ground nutmeg
1/4 teaspoon ground cinnamon
2 to 3 tablespoons apricot preserves
1/2 tablespoon water

Preheat oven to 375°. Grease or spray a 9-inch glass pie plate well. In a large bowl, mix the sliced pears, lemon juice, both sugars, honey, cornstarch, flour, and spices. Bring the apricot preserves and water to a boil. Stir hot preserves into pear mixture. Pour the pear mixture into the pie plate. Cover the pie with the pastry crust or the Apple Crisp Topping. Bake in preheated oven for 35 to 45 minutes or until the pears are cooked to the consistency you want.

Serves 8.

Note: If you are on a very low-fat diet, this pie can be made without either a pie crust or the topping. Just be sure to stir the pears once or twice while they are baking so they don't dry out.

Nutrition Values

Calories 227
Carbohydrates 43 gm
Cholesterol 0
Sodium 165 mg
Protein 1.8 gm
Total fat 6.3 gm
Polyunsaturated fat 1.6 gm
Monounsaturated fat 2.6 gm
Saturated fat 1.5 gm

Dietary fiber 3.8 gm
Percent of calories from
   Protein 3%
   Carbohydrates 73%
   Fat 24%
Exchanges
   1 bread
   1 fat
   1 1/2 fruit

PINEAPPLE CHEESE PIE

This pie may resemble a pineapple cheesecake in texture and taste, but that is where the comparison ends. Whereas a pineapple cheesecake is filled with cholesterol and saturated fat, this pie is bursting with flavor and healthy ingredients. Here is another dessert that will surprise everyone!

9-inch unbaked pastry crust
1 egg white, slightly beaten
16-ounce can of unsweetened crushed pineapple
6 tablespoon lowfat (1% or less) cottage cheese
2 tablespoons nonfat plain yogurt
2 tablespoons all-purpose unbleached flour
2 1/2 tablespoons brown sugar
2 tablespoons honey
1 teaspoon vanilla extract
1/4 teaspoon ground nutmeg or cardamon
4 large separated egg whites at room temperature
vegetable cooking spray

Preheat oven to 400°. Roll out the pie dough. Line the pie plate with the dough and prick the dough with a fork many times. Spray the shiny side of a piece of aluminum foil with vegetable cooking spray and place it over the dough—shiny side down. Fill the aluminum foil with pie weights, rice, beans, or a smaller pie plate. Bake for 8 to 10 minutes or until golden. Remove the foil and weights. Brush the dough with a slightly beaten egg white. Bake 3 to 5 minutes more and remove from oven. Lower the oven temperature to 325°.

Pies
● ● ● ● ● ● ● ● ● ● ● ● ● ● ● ● ●

Drain the pineapple for 15 minutes or more. In a food processor, using the steel blade, whip the cottage cheese and yogurt for at least 2 minutes or until completely smooth. Add the flour, sugar, honey, vanilla, and nutmeg. Whip for 1 minute. Add the 4 egg whites one at a time, and whip in between each addition. Remove the blade and stir in the pineapple. Pour the pineapple mixture into a partially baked pie crust. Bake in a low to moderate oven at 325° for 50 to 60 minutes. Too hot an oven causes ingredients to separate. Remove and let cool. Refrigerate and serve cold.

Serves 8.

Nutrition Values

Calories 180
Carbohydrates 27 gm
Cholesterol 0.5 mg
Sodium 245 mg
Protein 5.3 gm
Total fat 6 gm
Polyunsaturated fat 1.5 gm
Monounsaturated fat 2.5 gm
Saturated fat 1.5 gm
Dietary fiber 1.6 gm

Percent of calories from
Protein 12%
Carbohydrates 59%
Fat 30%
Exchanges
1 bread
1 fat
1/2 fruit
1/2 meat

PUMPKIN CHIFFON PIE

This is a lighter, healthier pumpkin pie than most.

9-inch unbaked pie shell
1 cup canned pumpkin
1 1/4 cups skim milk
1 tablespoon cornstarch
1/4 cup honey
2 tablespoons molasses
1 tablespoon packed brown sugar
1/4 teaspoon salt (optional)
1/4 teaspoon ground ginger
1/4 teaspoon ground nutmeg
1/2 teaspoon ground cinnamon
4 large egg whites at room temperature

Preheat oven to 350°. Place the pie shell into a pie plate.
Beat all the ingredients except the egg whites together. Set aside.
Wash and dry the beaters. Beat the egg whites until stiff and fold
into the pumpkin mixture. Pour into the pie shell. Bake for 1
hour or until set in preheated oven. Serve warm or cool.
Serves 8.

Nutrition Values

Calories 181
Carbohydrates 28 gm
Cholesterol 0.6 mg
Sodium 280 mg
Protein 4.7 gm
Total Fat 6 gm
Polyunsaturated fat 1.5 gm
Monounsaturated fat 2.5 gm
Saturated fat 1.5 gm

Dietary fiber 1.2 gm
Percent of calories from
Protein 10%
Carbohydrates 60%
Fat 29%
Exchanges
1 bread
1 fat
1/2 meat

PUMPKIN PIE

Try this healthier version of pumpkin pie. You won't miss the calories, cholesterol, or fat. If you are on a very low fat diet, you can even make this pie without the pie crust.

> 3 large egg whites at room temperature
> 16 ounces canned pumpkin
> 1/4 to 1/3 cup lightly packed brown sugar
> 1/4 cup maple syrup or molasses
> 3/4 teaspoon ground cinnamon
> 1/4 teaspoon ground ginger
> 1/4 teaspoon allspice
> 1 cup evaporated skim milk
> 9-inch unbaked pie crust in a pie plate

Preheat oven to 425°. Beat egg whites slightly. Beat in the pumpkin, brown sugar, maple syrup, cinnamon, ginger, allspice, and evaporated skim milk. Pour the mixture into the pie crust. Bake in preheated oven for 15 minutes. Reduce the temperature to 350°. Bake 35 to 40 minutes more or until a knife inserted near the center comes out clean.

Serves 8

Nutrition Values

Calories 203
Carbohydrates 33 gm
Cholesterol 1.3 mg
Sodium 227 mg
Protein 5.6 gm
Total fat 6 gm
Polyunsaturated fat 1.5 gm
Monounsaturated fat 2.5 gm
Saturated fat 1.6 gm

Dietary fiber 1.7 gm
Percent of calories from
    Protein 11%
    Carbohydrates 63%
    Fat 26%
Exchanges
    1 bread
    1 fat
    1/2 milk

STRAWBERRY PIE

This beautiful, light summer dessert will definitely be popular at your house.

> 10-inch baked pastry crust
> 1/2 cup lowfat (1% or less) cottage cheese
> 1 tablespoon nonfat plain yogurt
> 1 teaspoon fresh lemon juice
> 1 to 3 tablespoons confectioners' powdered sugar,
>   depending on desired sweetness
> 1 quart fresh strawberries, cleaned, hulled, and dried
> 3 tablespoons strawberry, apricot, or red currant jelly
> 1 tablespoon Cointreau, Grand Marnier (orange liqueur),
>   or orange juice

Using the steel blade, whirl the cottage cheese and yogurt in a food processor for 3 minutes or until completely smooth. Be sure to scrape the sides often. Add lemon juice and powdered sugar and whirl 60 seconds more. Spread cottage cheese mixture over prebaked, cooled pie crust. Cover this with the strawberries in an artistic design. You can use whole or sliced strawberries. Heat jelly over a low heat in small saucepan. Stir continually and do not let boil. When just below the boiling point, remove from heat and stir in orange liqueur or orange juice. When jelly glaze has cooled slightly, brush it on strawberries. Refrigerate and serve cold. **Serves 8.**

Note: Try this dessert using different berries and jellies. You can even combine some of these berries. If you want a dessert with less fat and calories, omit the pie crust. Spoon cottage cheese mixture on bottom of individual dessert dishes instead.

Nutrition Values

Calories 160
Carbohydrates 23 gm
Cholesterol 0.7 mg
Sodium 223 mg
Protein 3.6 gm
Total fat 6.2 gm
Polyunsaturated fat 1.6 gm
Monounsaturated fat 2.6 gm
Saturated fat 1.5 gm

Dietary fiber 2.5 gm
Percent of calories from
    Protein 9%
    Carbohydrates 55%
    Fat 34%
Exchanges
    1 bread, 1 fat
    1/2 fruit, 1/2 meat

TOP CRUST APPLE PIE

This recipe gives you all the taste of an old-fashioned apple pie with fewer calories and fat.

> 6 to 7 baking apples (I like to use a variety
>   of apples in each pie)
> 1/3 cup packed brown sugar
> 1 tablespoon honey
> 2 tablespoons flour
> 1 teaspoon lemon juice
> 1 teaspoon ground cinnamon
> 1/4 teaspoon freshly ground nutmeg
> 1/4 teaspoon vanilla extract
> 9-inch unbaked pie crust
> vegetable cooking spray

Preheat oven to 350°. Pare, core, and thinly slice apples. Mix sugar, honey, flour, lemon juice, cinnamon, nutmeg, and vanilla together. Add to apples and stir well. Spray a 9-inch glass pie dish with vegetable cooking spray. Fill pie dish with apple mixture. Cover with pie crust. Prick crust to allow the steam to escape. Bake 40 to 50 minutes. **Serves 8**

Nutrition Values

Calories 214
Carbohydrates 40 gm
Cholesterol 0
Sodium 166 mg
Protein 1.6 gm
Total fat 6.3 gm
Polyunsaturated fat 1.6 gm
Monounsaturated fat 2.5 gm
Saturated fat 1.5 gm

Dietary fiber 3.2 gm
Percent of calories from
 Protein 3%
 Carbohydrates 72%
 Fat 25%
Exchanges
 1 bread, 1 fat
 1 fruit

VEGETABLE OIL PIE CRUST

This pie crust has very little saturated fat and only a trace of cholesterol. Work the dough quickly so as not to activate the gluten. Try to keep the dough cold until you are ready to bake it. Do not add water to this crust.

1 cup minus 2 tablespoons sifted all-purpose enriched flour
1/2 cup stone-ground whole-wheat flour (If you want a
*   lighter-tasting crust, replace the whole-wheat*
*   flour with all-purpose flour)*
1 1/2 tablespoons cornstarch
1/4 cup canola oil, low-in-saturated-fat vegetable oil,
*   or light-tasting peanut oil*
1 tablespoon honey
2 to 3 tablespoons cold nonfat plain yogurt

Sift the dry ingredients together. Mix in the vegetable oil and honey. Quickly add just enough yogurt to hold the dough firmly together. Chill the dough for 10 minutes. Roll out the dough on a lightly floured piece of waxed paper. Make sure the rolling pin has been floured and remains so. If the dough is hard

to roll out, let it stand at room temperature for a few minutes.
When the circumference of the dough is one inch bigger than the
pie plate, invert the dough into a 9- or 10-inch pie plate. Carefully remove the waxed paper. You may choose to roll out the
dough before refrigerating it. If so, refrigerate the dough after it
has been put into the pie plate.

Nutrition Values

Calories 145
Carbohydrates 19 gm
Cholesterol 0.09 mg
Sodium 4.9 mg
Protein 2.3 gm
Total fat 7 gm
Polyunsaturated fat 2.3 gm
Monounsaturated fat 3.2 gm
Saturated fat 1.2 gm

Dietary fiber 1.2 gm
Percent of calories from
    Protein 6%
    Carbohydrates 51%
    Fat 43%
Exchanges
    1 bread
    1 1/2 fat

YOGURT CRUMB PIE TOPPING

I use this on top of fruit instead of a pie crust. If you prefer a lighter, whiter topping, use 5 tablespoons of all-purpose flour and omit the whole-wheat flour and oat bran.

3 tablespoons unbleached all-purpose flour
1 tablespoon stone-ground whole-wheat flour
1 tablespoon oat bran
1/2 teaspoon ground cinnamon
1/4 teaspoon ground nutmeg
1/4 cup lightly packed brown sugar
1 tablespoon honey
1 tablespoon vegetable oil or canola oil
1 tablespoon margarine
1/2 cup nonfat plain yogurt (optional)

Mix both flours, oat bran, cinnamon, nutmeg, brown sugar, and honey together. Cut in vegetable oil and margarine until a coarse meal forms. Spoon over prepared fruit. This makes a very tasty crumb topping. If you want to make a yogurt crumb topping, spread yogurt over top. Bake at 350° for 45 to 50 minutes.

Nutrition Values

Calories 84
Carbohydrates 13 gm
Cholesterol 0.3 mg
Sodium 30 mg
Protein 1.3 gm
Total fat 3.2 gm
Polyunsaturated fat 1 gm
Monounsaturated fat 1.4 gm
Saturated fFat 0.6 gm

Dietary fiber 0.3 gm
Percent of calories from
    Protein 6%
    Carbohydrates 60%
    Fat 34%
Exchanges
    1/2 Fat

Pies
• • • • • • • • • • • • • • • • •

YOGURT PIE

This was one of the first recipes I created for this book. My husband's love for cheesecake inspired it. Not actually a pie, this yogurt dessert will satisfy even the most avid cheesecake lover. Be sure to start this dessert 24 hours before you want to serve it.

1 quart (32 ounces) nonfat plain yogurt
(I have best results with Colombo® Nonfat Yogurt)
2 large egg whites at room temperature
1/2 cup granulated sugar
1/2 teaspoon vanilla extract
1/2 teaspoon lemon extract
1 tablespoon cornstarch
vegetable cooking spray

Line a colander with cheesecloth. Fill the colander with the yogurt. Place the colander over a bowl so the yogurt can drain while refrigerated for at least 12 hours. Discard drained liquid.
Preheat oven to 350°. Spray a 9-inch glass pie plate with vegetable cooking spray. Beat egg whites until soft peaks form. Beat in sugar, vanilla, lemon extract, and cornstarch. Beat in drained yogurt. Pour this into the prepared pie plate and bake for 30 to 35 minutes or until firm. Refrigerate and serve cold.

Serves 8

Let Them Eat Cake
●●●●●●●●●●●●●●●●●

Nutrition Values

Calories 117
Carbohydrates 22 gm
Cholesterol 2 mg
Sodium 101 mg
Protein 7.4 gm
Total fat 0.2 gm
Polyunsaturated fat 0 gm
Monounsaturated fat 0 gm

Saturated fat 0.1 gm
Dietary Fiber 0 gm
Percent of calories from
   Protein 25%
   Carbohydrates 74%
   Fat 2%
Exchanges
   1/2 bread, 1 milk

ABOUT SAVORY PUDDINGS AND COLD DESSERTS

Even though you are controlling your saturated fat and cholesterol consumption, you don't have to give up these creamy confections. You can still enjoy the smooth, creamy taste of a delicious pudding without worrying about damaging your heart. The taste of these desserts will bring back childhood memories, when no one thought about cholesterol or saturated fat.

You can serve these desserts at the most elegant dinner party or you can serve them in a more casual setting. Your children will love them. Everyone loves them. Whenever you serve them you can be sure that you aren't doing damage to anyone's health or heart. You'll have to remind yourself of this because your taste buds will cause you to doubt it, but the proof is in the pudding.

APPLE RICE PUDDING

The apples are a perfect complement to this rice pudding.
They keep the pudding moist and rich tasting without adding
unnecessary fat.

1 1/4 cups water
1 1/4 cups skim milk
1/4 to 1/2 cup granulated sugar
1/4 teaspoon salt (optional)
1 cup raw white rice
6 large apples
1 teaspoon lemon juice
1/2 cup cup raisins (optional)
1/4 cup granulated sugar
1/4 cup brown sugar
1/2 teaspoon ground cinnamon
1/4 teaspoon freshly ground nutmeg
2 large egg whites
1 teaspoon vanilla extract
vegetable cooking spray

Topping:

Mix together:
        1 tablespoon granulated sugar
        1 tablespoon brown sugar
        1 teaspoon ground cinnamon

Preheat oven to 350°. Spray a 9- x 13-inch pan with vegetable cooking spray. In a medium saucepan, heat the water and milk until just under the boiling point. Remove the saucepan from the heat and stir in 1/2 cup sugar, the salt, and the rice. Cover, return to heat, and simmer for 20 to 25 minutes or until rice is tender. Remove from heat and let cool a little.

Peel and core the apples and cut them into small cubes. Sprinkle them with lemon juice to keep them from turning brown and stir in the raisins. Mix the granulated sugar, brown sugar, cinnamon, and nutmeg together. Stir this mixture into the apples. Beat the egg whites until light and frothy. Beat in the vanilla. Stir the egg whites into the cooled rice and then mix in the apple mixture. Pour this into the prepared pan, spread it out evenly, and sprinkle it with the cinnamon sugar topping. Cover the pan with aluminum foil and bake for 15 minutes. Uncover and bake an additional 15 minutes. Serve this warm or reheat after refrigerating.

Serves 12.

Nutrition Values

Calories 199
Carbohydrates 48 gm
Cholesterol 0.4 gm
Sodium 71 mg
Protein 2.9 gm
Total fat 0.5 gm
Polyunsaturated fat 0.1 gm
Monounsaturated fat 0.05 gm
Saturated fat 0.1 gm

Dietary fiber 2 gm
Percent of calories from
    Protein 6%
    Carbohydrates 92%
    Fat 2%
Exchanges
    1 bread
    1 fruit

BREAD PUDDING

I visited a restaurant in New Orleans a few years ago and fell in love with their bread pudding. I have taken their ingredients and modified them to fit into a low-fat and low-cholesterol diet. Try to use day-old French bread when making this dessert. It makes the pudding not only more authentic but also more delicious.

1 loaf day-old French bread about 1 1/2 feet long
1 quart skim milk
2 large egg whites and 1 whole egg beaten together
1/2 cup brown sugar, lightly packed
1/2 cup honey
2 teaspoons vanilla extract
1 1/2 teaspoons ground cinnamon
1 tablespoon canola oil
2 teaspoons Butter Buds® (natural dehydrated butter)
1/2 cup raisins
vegetable cooking spray

Preheat oven to 350°. Spray a 9- x 13- inch pan with vegetable cooking spray. Tear the bread into bite size pieces and place in a large bowl. Cover with milk and let stand for 1 hour, stirring occasionally. Beat the eggs, brown sugar, honey, vanilla, cinnamon, canola oil, and Butter Buds together. Stir this mixture into the soaked bread. Mix in the raisins. Pour the pudding into the pan and bake for one hour or until set well. Do not dry out the pudding. Serve warm with maple syrup sauce.
Serves 12.

Maple Syrup Sauce

1/4 cup pure maple syrup
1 teaspoon Butter Buds® (natural dehydrated butter)
1 tablespoon cornstarch
1 cup skim milk
1/8 teaspoon freshly ground nutmeg
1/2 teaspoon vanilla extract
2 tablespoons bourbon

Place the maple syrup, Butter Buds, and cornstarch in a small saucepan. Stir well. Add milk and bring just to the boiling point while stirring over medium heat. Lower the heat and simmer until thickened, stirring constantly. Remove from heat. Stir in nutmeg, vanilla, and bourbon. Serve warm over pudding.

Nutrition Values

Calories 274
Carbohydrates 51 gm
Cholesterol 19.4 gm
Sodium 303 mg
Protein 8.7 gm
Total fat 3.4 gm
Polyunsaturated fat 0.9 gm
Monounsaturated fat 1.2 gm
Saturated fat 0.7 gm
Dietary fiber 1.3 gm

Percent of calories from
Protein 13%
Carbohydrates 74%
Fat 11%
Exchanges
1 1/2 bread
1/2 fat
1/2 fruit
1/2 milk

COEUR A LA CREME

I love to serve this dessert at dinner parties because everyone is sure they are eating something sinfully rich. This dessert is very elegant, but you don't have to feel guilty about serving it. It needs to be prepared a day in advance, however.

> 1 1/2 cups lowfat (1% or less) large-curd cottage cheese
> 1 cup lowfat ricotta cheese
> 1/4 cup skim milk or nonfat plain yogurt
> 2 to 4 tablespoons confectioners' powdered sugar
> 1/2 teaspoon vanilla extract
> 1/2 cup lemon water (1/2 cup water and juice of 1/2 lemon
>   mixed together)
> 6 ounces raspberries, fresh or frozen
> 2 teaspoons Kirsch
> 1 tablespoon red currant preserves

Using steel blade, process cottage cheese, ricotta cheese, milk or yogurt, powdered sugar, and vanilla in food processor at highest speed for 2 minutes or until completely smooth. Dip cheesecloth in lemon water. Squeeze cloth well. Line strainer with cheesecloth. Pour cheese mixture into strainer. Place strainer over a bowl so cheese mixture can drip into it while refrigerated for at least 12 hours. Discard liquid in bowl.

Puree raspberries in food processor. Press raspberries through sieve and discard seeds. Mix raspberries with Kirsch and currant preserves. Spoon out drained cheese mixture into individual dessert bowls. Cover each bowl with raspberry sauce. Serve immediately.

Serves 6 to 8.

Nutrition Values

Calories 149
Carbohydrates 15 gm
Cholesterol 15.3 gm
Sodium 289 mg
Protein 12.5 gm
Total fat 4 gm
Polyunsaturated fat 0.2 gm
Monounsaturated fat 1.1 gm
Saturated fat 2.4 gm

Dietary fiber 1.3 gm
Percent of calories from
   Protein 34%
   Carbohydrates 40%
   Fat 24%
Exchanges
   1/2 fat
   2 meat

CREAMY CHEESE MOUSSE

This is a delightfully light dessert that will fool all of your guests. They will be sure that they are eating something terribly rich and fattening. You don't need to tell them they are mistaken.

2 envelopes unflavored gelatin
1/2 cup cold water
1 1/2 cups nonfat milk
1/4 cup honey
1/3 cup flour
16 ounces lowfat (1% or less) small curd cottage cheese
3/4 teaspoon vanilla extract
1/2 teaspoon almond extract
3 large egg whites at room temperature
1/3 cup sugar
1 pint pureed fresh or frozen strawberries
   or pureed, strained raspberries
vegetable cooking spray

Sprinkle the gelatin over the water. Mix and let soften for about 5 minutes. Heat milk over medium heat. Stir in the honey and sprinkle in the flour. Stir until thick. Add the softened gelatin. Stir until it is dissolved. Cook one more minute over low heat. Set aside to cool. Using steel blade in food processor, beat the cottage cheese for 3 minutes until it is totally smooth. Beat in the vanilla and almond extract. Beat in the milk/gelatin mixture. Beat one more minute. In a large bowl, beat the egg whites with an electric beater until they are foamy. While still beating, gradually add the sugar until stiff peaks form. Fold the egg whites into the cottage cheese mixture. Spray a 6-cup mold with vegetable cooking spray. Fill the mold with the cottage cheese mixture and refrigerate at least 6 hours or until the mousse is totally firm. Unmold the mousse and cover with pureed strawberries or raspberries sweetened to your taste. This mousse unmolds very easily.

Serves 8.

Nutrition Values

Calories 161
Carbohydrates 27 gm
Cholesterol 3.3 gm
Sodium 278 mg
Protein 12 gm
Total fat 0.8 gm
Polyunsaturated fat 0.1 gm
Monounsaturated fat 0.2 gm
Saturated fat 0.4 gm

Dietary fiber 1.1 gm
Percent of calories from
    Protein 30%
    Carbohydrates 66%
    Fat 5%
Exchanges
    1 meat
    1/2 milk

ENGLISH RICE CREAM

This English rice cream is much lighter and creamier than rice pudding. I have taken this English favorite and modified it to fit into a low-fat and low-cholesterol diet. I'm sure that this will become an American favorite.

1/4 cup raw white rice
1 cup nonfat milk
1 tablespoon honey
1 tablespoon granulated sugar
1/2 teaspoon vanilla extract
1 teaspoon unflavored gelatin
2 large egg whites at room temperature
1 tablespoon powdered sugar
1/2 cup nonfat milk
raspberries, blueberries, or sliced strawberries
sweetened to taste

Combine rice, milk, honey, sugar, and vanilla extract in small heavy saucepan. Cover, stir, and cook over a medium-low heat for 40 minutes or until rice is soft. Stir regularly. Remove pan from heat. Sprinkle the gelatin on the rice and stir until dissolved. Cool rice to room temperature.

Beat egg whites until soft peaks form. Beat in the powdered sugar. Slowly beat in the milk. Stir this into the rice. Pour the rice mixture into food processor and process with steel blade for 1 to 2 minutes. Pour the rice cream into individual dessert bowls or glasses. Chill until set. To serve, top with fruit of your choice.
Serves 4 to 6.

Nutrition Values

Calories 126
Carbohydrates 24 gm
Cholesterol 1.5 gm
Sodium 77 mg
Protein 7 gm
Total fat 0.3 gm
Polyunsaturated fat 0.1 gm
Monounsaturated fat 0.1 gm
Saturated fat 0.1 gm

Dietary fiber 0.5 gm
Percent of calories from
   Protein 22%
   Carbohydrates 76%
   Fat 2%
Exchanges
   1 bread
   1/2 milk
   1/2 meat

KEY LIME YOGURT PUDDING

This versatile dessert has a fresh, tart taste. It is great as a pudding and is equally as delicious when used as a pie filling. Just use a baked pastry crust that has been cooled and you have a lovely key lime yogurt pie to serve.

1/2 to 3/4 cup sugar
3 tablespoons honey
2 tablespoons cornstarch
1/4 cup lime juice (about 4 limes)
1 tablespoon grated lime peel
1 envelope unflavored gelatin
2 tablespoons cold water
1 cup lowfat (1%) cottage cheese
1 cup plain nonfat yogurt
vegetable cooking spray

Spray a 6-cup mold with vegetable cooking spray. In a small saucepan, heat the sugar, honey, cornstarch, lime juice, and 2 teaspoons of the grated lime peel until smooth and thick. Stir constantly. Set aside. In a small bowl, sprinkle the gelatin over the water. Let stand 5 minutes or until completely absorbed. Meanwhile, whip the cottage cheese in a food processor for 3 minutes or until completely smooth. Be sure to scrape the sides of the food processor. Add the yogurt and whip 1 more minute. Keep this mixture in the food processor. Pour the dissolved gelatin into the heated lime mixture. Heat and stir until completely dissolved—about 2 minutes over medium heat. Remove from heat and let cool slightly. Stir this into the whipped cottage cheese/yogurt mixture and process on high for 30 seconds. Pour into the prepared mold or individual dessert bowls. Sprinkle with remaining lime rind. Chill until set.

Serves 6.

Nutrition Values

Calories 189
Carbohydrates 40 gm
Cholesterol 2.3 gm
Sodium 185 mg
Protein 8 gm
Total fat 0.5 gm
Polyunsaturated fat 0.02 gm
Monounsaturated fat 0.1 gm
Saturated fat 0.3 gm

Dietary fiber 0.05 gm
Percent of calories from
   Protein 16%
   Carbohydrates 82%
   Fat 2%
Exchanges
   1/2 milk
   1 meat

LEMON PUDDING

Lemon lovers will adore this pudding. It is delightful to eat and easy to make. I recommend using one whole egg to prevent curdling. The pudding will separate while baking into a light upper crust and a creamy bottom.

1/4 cup honey
1 tablespoon canola oil
1 tablespoon light cream cheese
1/3 cup all-purpose unbleached flour
1 whole large egg, separated
2 teaspoons grated lemon rind
1/4 teaspoon lemon extract
1/4 cup fresh lemon juice
1 1/2 cups skim milk
2 egg whites at room temperature
1/8 teaspoon cream of tartar
1/4 cup granulated sugar
vegetable cooking spray

Preheat oven to 325°. Spray a 1 1/2-quart glass baking dish with vegetable cooking pray. Cream honey, canola oil, and cream cheese together. Stir in flour and then mix in egg yolk. Add lemon rind, lemon extract, lemon juice, and skim milk and stir well. In another bowl, beat 2 egg whites plus the separated egg white with cream of tartar until soft peaks form. Beat in sugar 1 tablespoon at a time. Fold egg whites into batter. Pour batter into prepared baking dish and set dish into a larger dish. Fill larger dish halfway with boiling water. Bake 1 hour. Serve warm or cold. **Serves 6.**

Nutrition Values

Calories 163
Carbohydrates 28 gm
Cholesterol 37.3 gm
Sodium 75 mg
Protein 5 gm
Total fat 3.7 gm
Polyunsaturated fat 0.8 gm
Monounsaturated fat 1.4 gm
Saturated fat 1 gm
Dietary fiber 0.2 gm

Percent of calories from
  Protein 12%
  Carbohydrates 68%
  Fat 20%
Exchanges
  1 bread
  1/2 fat

STRAWBERRY MOUSSE

This is a delightful dessert, sure to please everyone. By definition, it is not exactly a mousse, but its light texture resembles that of a rich, creamy mousse. Try using peaches for a completely different taste.

1 package unflavored gelatin
1/4 cup water
1/4 cup nonfat milk
1/3 cup granulated sugar
1 cup lowfat (1%) cottage cheese
1 quart fresh strawberries, cleaned, hulled, and dried
1 tablespoon orange liqueur (optional)
4 large egg whites at room temperature
2 tablespoons granulated sugar
vegetable cooking spray

Spray a 6-cup mold with vegetable cooking spray. Sprinkle the gelatin over the water and let stand for 5 minutes. Heat milk over medium heat. Just before the boiling point is reached, stir in

1/3 cup sugar and the gelatin. Continue heating and stirring until gelatin is dissolved but don't let the mixture boil. Remove from heat and set aside. Using steel blade, whip the cottage cheese in the food processor for 3 minutes or until it is completely smooth. Be sure to scrape the sides of the food processor often. Add the strawberries and whip 1 more minute or until everything is pureed. Add the orange liqueur and gelatin mixture. Whip 1 minute more. In a medium bowl, beat the egg whites until soft peaks form. While beating, slowly add 2 tablespoons of sugar until stiff peaks form. Slowly stir the strawberry mixture into the egg whites. Pour into the prepared mold and chill until set. Unmold and serve.

Serves 8.

Nutrition Values

Calories 104
Carbohydrates 18 gm
Cholesterol 1.4 gm
Sodium 148 mg
Protein 7 gm
Total fat 0.6 gm
Polyunsaturated fat 0.2 gm
Monounsaturated fat 0.1 gm
Saturated fat 0.2 gm

Dietary fiber 2 gm
Percent of calories from
Protein 25%
Carbohydrates 67%
Fat 5%
Exchanges
1/2 fruit
1 meat

SUMMER FRUIT MOUSSE

I usually use kiwis for this delightfully creamy dessert, but there are many types of fruits equally delicious.

Choose one of the following fruits:
6 to 7 kiwis, or 1 1/2 pints of strawberries,
or 1 1/2 pounds of nectarines,
or 1 1/2 pounds of peaches
1/2 cup granulated sugar
1/2 cup water
1 cup lowfat (1% or less) cottage cheese
1/2 cup nonfat plain yogurt
1 to 2 tablespoons honey
1/4 cup fresh lemon juice
1 envelope plus 1 1/2 teaspoons unflavored gelatin
1/4 cup Grand Marnier, Cointreau, or Peach Schnapps
vegetable cooking spray

Spray a 6-cup mold with vegetable cooking spray. Peel and chop kiwi, or hull and clean strawberries, or peel, pit, and chop nectarines or peaches. Combine fruit with 1/2 cup sugar and 1/2 cup water. Bring mixture to a boil. Simmer 15 minutes. Cool slightly.

Put cottage cheese and yogurt in food processor. Using steel blade, whip the cottage cheese and yogurt for 3 minutes on high. Be sure to scrape the sides often. Pour in the cooked and cooled fruit mixture and whip for 60 seconds. Add the honey, check for sweetness, and whip for 10 seconds. Leave mixture in food processor.

Pour lemon juice into small saucepan. Sprinkle gelatin over lemon juice. Let soften 5 minutes. Heat gelatin mixture over low heat until dissolved. Let cool slightly. Pour gelatin mixture and liqueur into food processor. Process for 60 seconds. Pour everything into prepared mold and refrigerate 4 hours or until firm. Unmold mousse and serve cold.

Serves 8.

Nutrition Values

Calories 139
Carbohydrates 26 gm
Cholesterol 1.5 gm
Sodium 129 mg
Protein 6 gm
Total fat 0.5 gm
Polyunsaturated fat 0.1 gm
Monounsaturated fat 0.1 gm

Saturated Fat 0.2 gm
Dietary fiber 1.5 gm
Percent of calories from
    Protein 17%
    Carbohydrates 71%
    Fat 3%
Exchanges
    1/2 fruit, 1/2 meat

TRIFLE

I am sure you are surprised to see this in a low-fat, low-cholesterol cookbook. As you can see from the ingredients, though, even a dessert as rich as a trifle can be transformed into something healthier.

1 low-fat yellow cake or low-fat sponge cake
3 cups nonfat milk
1/4 to 1/2 cup granulated sugar (depending
*   on desired sweetness)*
4 tablespoons cornstarch
1 teaspoon vanilla extract
1/3 to 1/2 cup fresh orange juice
1 to 2 tablespoons Grand Marnier orange liqueur, (optional)
1/2 to 2/3 cup raspberry jam
raspberries or sliced strawberries to garnish

Puddings and Cold Desserts

Make the pudding by heating 2 1/2 cups milk and the sugar just to boiling point. Stir constantly. Lower the heat and keep the milk from boiling. Mix the cornstarch and the remaining 1/2 cup of milk together to make a paste. Mix the cornstarch paste into the hot milk. While stirring, let the milk mixture simmer but not boil for 2 to 4 minutes or until you can no longer taste the cornstarch. (If you are concerned about burning the milk, you can use the top of a double boiler placed over boiling water to heat the milk. This process takes longer, about 8 to 10 minutes.) Stir in the vanilla and remove from the heat. Let cool. Depending on the size of the cake, you may not need to use all of the pudding.

Use your prettiest clear glass large serving bowl and spread about 1/4 of a cup of the pudding all over the bottom of the bowl. Place half the cake into the bowl. (The cake can be cut into pieces to fit the shape of the bowl.) Mix the orange juice and orange liqueur together. Sprinkle half of the orange juice mixture over the cake. Spread half of the jam onto the cake. Pour half of the pudding over the cake. Cover with the remaining cake, orange juice, jam, and pudding. Garnish with the sliced fruit. Refrigerate until cold.

Serves 10 to 12.

Note: For an added taste and color, try adding some sliced straw-berries in between the cake layers.

Nutrition Values

Calories 293
Carbohydrates 62 gm
Cholesterol 29 gm
Sodium 281 mg
Protein 5 gm
Total fat 2.6 gm
Polyunsaturated fat 0.01 gm
Monounsaturated fat 0.04 gm
Saturated fat 0.9 gm

Dietary fiber 0.3 gm
Percent of calories from
  Protein 7%
  Carbohydrates 84%
  Fat 8%
Exchanges
  2 bread, 1/2 fat
  1/2 milk

Let Them Eat Cake
●●●●●●●●●●●●●●●●●●

SELECTED BIBLIOGRAPHY

Anderson, James. "Hypocholesterolemic Effects of Oat or Bean Products." Presentation at the First International Congress on Vegetarian Nutrition, Washington, D.C., March 16, 1987.

Brand, David. "Searching for Life's Elixir." *Time,* December 12, 1988, pp. 62-65.

Brody, Jane E. "Fats and Oils, How to Choose, Which to Use." *Family Circle,* March 15, 1988, pp. 154-156.

Brody, Jane E. *Jane Brody's Good Food Book.* New York: Bantam Books, 1987.

Brody, Jane E. *Jane Brody's Nutrition Book.* New York: Bantam Books, 1987.

Center for Science in the Public Interest. *Nutrition Action Healthletters.* Washington D.C.: CSPI, 1991.

Clark, Matt; Gosnell, Mary; Hager, Mary; Carroll, Ginny; and Gordon, Jeanne. "What You Should Know About Heart Attacks." *Newsweek*, February 8, 1988, pp. 50-54.

Clark, Matt; Hager, Mary; Drew, Lisa; and King, Patricia. *"Controlling Cholesterol."* Newsweek, October 19, 1987, pp. 94-97.

Connor, Sonja L., and Connor, William E. *The New American Diet.* New York: Simon and Schuster, 1986.

Cooper, Kenneth. *Controlling Cholesterol.* New York: Bantam Books, 1988.

Let Them Eat Cake

Editorial Board, University of California at Berkley. *University of California Wellness Letters.* Florida: School of Public Health and Health Letter Association, 1990-1991.

Fisher, Hans, and Boe, Eugene. *The Rutgers Guide to Lowering Your Cholesterol.* New Jersey: Rutgers University Press, 1985.

Gasner, Douglas, and McCleary, Elliot. *The American Medical Association Book of Heartcare.* New York: Random House, 1982.

Gershoff, Stanley N., ed. *Tufts University Diet and Nutrition Letters.* Boston: Tufts Diet and Nutrition Letter, 1989-1990.

Goldbeck, Nikki and David. *Nikki and David Goldbeck's American Wholefoods Cuisine.* New York: New American Library, 1983.

Grady, Denise. "Can Heart Disease Be Reversed?" *Discover,* March, 1987, pp. 55-68.

Greater Cincinnati Nutrition Council. "Food for Thought." Cincinnati, Ohio: January/February, 1988, pp. 1-4.

Griffin, Glen, and Castelli, William. *Good Fat, Bad Fat, How to Lower Cholesterol and Beat the Odds of a Heart Attack.* Tucson, AZ: Fisher Books, 1989.

Grundy, Scott M. "Cholesterol and Coronary Heart Disease." *Journal of the American Medical Association,* Volume 264, No. 23 (December 19, 1990), pp. 3053-3058.

"Heart Health." *Newsweek,* February 13, 1989, pp. S4-S18.

Horovitz, Emmanuel. *Cholesterol Control Made Easy.* Los

Bibliography

Angeles: Health Trend Publishing, 1990.

Journal of the American Medical Association. Editorial, Volume 264, No. 23 (December 19, 1990), pp. 3060-3061.

Karmally, Wahida. "Shopping and Cooking Your Way to a Lower Cholesterol Level." *Newsweek*, November 7, 1988, pp. S6-S20.

Kolata, Gina. "Major Study Aims to Learn Who Should Lower Cholesterol." *The New York Times,* September 26, 1989.

Kolata, Gina. "New Theory Explains How Cholesterol Threatens the Heart." *The New York Times,* October 25, 1988.

Kowalski, Robert E. *Cholesterol and Children.* New York: Harper and Row, 1988.

Kwiterovich, Peter. *Beyond Cholesterol, The Johns Hopkins Complete Guide for Avoiding Heart Disease.* Baltimore: The Johns Hopkins University Press, 1989.

Lauer, Ronald, and Clarke, William. "Use of Cholesterol Measurements in Childhood for the Prediction of Adult Hypercholesterolemia." *Journal of the American Medical Association*, Volume 264, No. 23, (December 19, 1990), pp. 3034-3038.

Leblang, Bonnie Tandy. "Spread Yourself Thin." *American Health,* September, 1991, pp. 45-47.

Mazzeo-Caputo, Stephanie. "Heart Healthy Eating." *Newsweek,* February 13, 1989, pp. S12-S15.

Monmaney, Terence; Springen, Karen; Hager, Mary; and

Shapiro, Daniel. "The Cholesterol Connection." *Newsweek*, February 8, 1988, pp. 56-58.

National Cholesterol Education Program. *Report of the Expert Panel on Detection, Evaluation, and Treatment of High Blood Cholesterol in Adults*, 1987.

Newman, Thomas B.; Browner, Warren S.; and Hulley, Stephen B. "The Case Against Childhood Cholesterol Screening." *Journal of the American Medical Association*, Volume 264, No. 23. (December 19, 1990), pp. 3039-3042.

Ornish, Dean. *Stress, Diet, and Your Heart*. New York: New American Library, 1982.

Piscatella, Joseph. *Choices for a Healthy Heart*. New York: Workman Publishing, 1987.

Pritikin, Robert. *The New Pritikin Program: The Easy and Delicious Way to Shed Fat, Lower Your Cholesterol, and Stay Fit*. New York: Simon and Schuster, 1990.

Purdy, Susan G. *Basic Apple to Four and Twenty Blackbirds, It's as Easy as Pie*. New York: Atheneum, 1984.

Rombauer, Irma S., and Becker, Marion Rombauer. *Joy of Cooking*. Indianapolis, Indiana: The Bobbs-Merrill Company, 1969.

Roth, Eli M., and Streicher, Sandra L. *Good Cholesterol, Bad Cholesterol*. Rocklin, CA: Prima Publishing and Communications, 1989.

Shapiro, Laura; Koehl, Carla; Springen, Karen; Manly, Howard;

Bibliography

Pyrillis, Rita; Hager, Mary; and Starr, Mark. "Feeding Frenzy." *Newsweek,* May 27, 1991. pp. 46-53.

Ulene, Art. *Count Out Cholesterol, American Medical Association Campaign Against Cholesterol.* New York: Feeling Fine Programs and Alfred A. Knopf, Inc., 1989.

Waldholz, Michael. "Lab Notes." *The Wall Street Journal,* August 8, 1991.

"What You Should Know About Heart Attacks." *Newsweek on Health,* Summer, 1988, pp. 8-18.

Let Them Eat Cake
● ● ● ● ● ● ● ● ● ● ● ● ● ● ● ●

INDEX

Let Them Eat Cake

Index

Let Them Eat Cake

Index

CHRONIMED Publishing Books of Related Interest

60 Days of Low-Fat, Low-Cost Meals in Minutes by M.J. Smith, R.D., L.D., M.A. Following the path of the best-seller *All American Low-Fat Meals in Minutes,* here are more than 150 quick and sumptuous recipes complete with the latest exchange values and nutrition facts for lowering calories, fat, salt, and cholesterol. This book contains complete menus for 60 days and recipes that use only ingredients found in virtually any grocery store—most for a total cost of less than $10.
004205, ISBN 1-56561-010-5 $12.95

All-American Low-Fat Meals in Minutes by M.J. Smith, R.D., L.D., M.A. Filled with tantalizing recipes and valuable tips, this cookbook makes great-tasting low-fat foods a snap for holidays, special occasions, or everyday. Most recipes take only minutes to prepare.
004079, ISBN 0-937721-73-5 $12.95

The Guiltless Gourmet by Judy Gilliard and Joy Kirkpatrick, R.D. A perfect fusion of sound nutrition and creative cooking, this book is loaded with delicious recipes high in flavor and low in fat, sugar, calories, cholesterol, and salt.
004021, ISBN 0-937721-23-9 $9.95

The Guiltless Gourmet Goes Ethnic by Judy Gilliard and Joy Kirkpatrick, R.D. More than a cookbook, this sequel to *The Guiltless Gourmet* shows how easy it is to lower the sugar, calories, sodium, and fat in your favorite ethnic dishes—without sacrificing taste.
004072, ISBN 0-937721-68-9 $11.95

European Cuisine from the Guiltless Gourmet by Judy Gilliard and Joy Kirkpatrick, R.D. This book shows you how to lower the sugar, salt, cholesterol, total fat, and calories in delicious Greek, English, German, Russian, and Scandinavian dishes. Plus it features complete nutrition information and the latest exchange values.
004085, ISBN 0-937721-81-6 $11.95

The Joy of Snacks by Nancy Cooper, R.D. Offers more than 200 delicious recipes and nutrition information for hearty snacks, including sandwiches, appetizers, soups, spreads, cookies, muffins, and treats especially for kids. The book also suggests guidelines for selecting convenience snacks and interpreting information on food labels.
004086, ISBN 0-937721-82-4 $12.95

Convenience Food Facts by Marion Franz, R.D., M.S., and Arlene Monk, R.D., C.D.E. Includes complete nutrition information, tips, and exchange values on more than 1,500 popular name-brand processed foods commonly found in grocery store freezers and shelves. Helps you plan easy-to-prepare, nutritious meals.
004081, ISBN 0-937721-77-8 $10.95

Fast Food Facts by Marion Franz, R.D., M.S. This revised and up-to-date best-seller shows how to make smart nutrition choices at fast food restaurants—and tells what to avoid. Includes complete nutrition information on more than 1,000 menu offerings from the 21 largest fast food chains.

Standard-size edition	004068, ISBN 0-937721-67-0	$6.95
Pocket edition	004073, ISBN 0-937721-69-7	$4.95

Exchanges for All Occasions by Marion Franz, R.D., M.S. Exchanges and meal planning suggestions for just about any occasion, sample meal plans, special tips for people with diabetes, and more.
004003, ISBN 0-937721-22-0 $8.95